Royal Babylon

Other books by Heathcote Williams:
The Speakers; The Local Stigmatic; AC/DC;
The Immortalist; Hancock's Last Half Hour;
Whale Nation; Sacred Elephant; Falling for
a Dolphin; Autogeddon; Forbidden Fruit;
Shelley at Oxford; Badshah Khan: Islamic
Peace Warrior

Royal Babylon

Heathcote Williams

First published 2016 by
Skyscraper Publications
Talton Edge, Newbold on Stour,
Warks CV37 8TR, U.K.
www.skyscraperpublications.com

A CIP catalogue record for this book is available
from the British Library.

ISBN-13: 978-1-911072-00-3

Cover concept and design by
Buchgut, Berlin

Typeset by
Chandler Book Design

Printed and bound in Great Britain by
Latitude Press

Royal Babylon:

The Criminal Record of the British Monarchy

AN INVESTIGATIVE POEM

By
Heathcote Williams

*"The comfort of the rich depends upon an
abundant supply of the poor."*

VOLTAIRE

In 1840, Pierre-Joseph Proudhon the first self-declared
anarchist, defined anarchy in *'What is Property?'*, as "the
absence of a master, of a sovereign".

Royal Babylon

In the year of the Queen's Silver Jubilee tourists peered as usual
Through the railings of Buckingham Palace,
But her fairy tale was fading; the fairy queen's wings were being clipped
By the Sex Pistols putting monarchy in their sights.

"God save the queen," they sang, "it's a fascist regime."
And the song's hook-line became a new anthem;
Disturbing to clutches of flag-wavers lining the streets
And horrifying to Middle England and the *Daily Mail*.

The Sex Pistols proclaimed, *"She ain't no human being,"*
And the subversive posters for their record
Placed the band's salacious name right across the Queen's lips,
And they masked her eyes with two spidery swastikas.

They sang, *"I don't believe illusions 'cos too much is real"*.
They accessorized the Queen's nose with safety pins
Like a voodoo doll, and covered her face with cutout letters
As if presenting the world with a kidnapper's note.

'Oooh no,' people would say, 'you can't have a go at the Queen,'
Sucking their breath in to indicate caution,
'Oooh no, not the Queen, the Queen's above politics you see.'
'They can't answer back, can they, so it's not fair.'

Then they'd earnestly claim, 'It's in the constitution, isn't it?'
Forgetting that Britain's never had such a document –
For the Brits, despite their inordinate pride in their own history,
Often reveal they know less about it than anyone.

The country survives despite its own past not because of it.
Its infantile wish for a benign parent above politics
Persuades it to ignore unpleasant facts, such as the sovereign's endorsing
The nastiest political act of all, namely killing.

For their sovereign's dominant role is to inspect
Row after row of the state's armed forces:
Broken down in training, reconfigured from scratch
Then programmed to kill on command.

The sovereign's crucial to the lubrication of Britain's wars
By its gulling soldiers into dutifully dying;
Then, after paying homage to these victims of state carnage,
By its encouraging arms-trade profiteering.

The arms makers and their customers are brought together
At Windsor Castle to be honoured with fly-pasts –
Monarchy and military business being intimately connected.
The UK's 'Defence Industrial Base' is a royal brand.

A landowning cabal with its heraldry denoting privilege
Still forms an elite network staking out the country's land.
They retain monarchy as their god to deceive those who live here,
Whose common land they once stole and enclosed.

The monarchy's militarism echoes a time when royalty wasn't flouted —
When querying royalty was treason and when those threatening
The status quo could be seized, and their limbs tied to horses
Which took off in every direction as they were whipped.

On seeing royal victims torn to shreds while still alive,
Royal minions sliced their hearts into sections
Then sent them across the whole country for public display
And a warning to anyone considering rebellion.

In the past, the brute power of the monarchy was quite unrestrained
Whereas it now pretends to behave with more decorum:
By dressing in fancy costumes, and awarding itself unearned medals,
And laying wreaths to those who die in its name.

It's genteel, but its politicized charisma still yields a body-count:
Lives are still culled by the 'Queen and Country' spell.
Royalty pays off its dead subjects with a march-past and their reward
Is to have their remains returned in a box to where they lived.

Meanwhile royalty's own patriotism bears scant inspection:
It being revealed in 1915, in World War One,
That when millions were dying in Flanders for King and Country,
The King himself was tobogganing in St Moritz.

He'd also set a wartime record for shooting Sandringham pheasants
And he'd cut his regular swathe through its wildlife;
Likewise, in 1939, King George VI would fret that the war
Would "interrupt the grouse season at Balmoral".

The UK's military-monarchy complex is a cynical industry
For which the Queen was groomed by a General Browning
And, likewise, Prince William's mentor has been Blair's wartime apparatchik:
The UK's former man in Washington, David Manning.

"It is Manning who is running the conflict with Iraq,"
Wrote John Kampfner, the author of 'Blair's Wars'.
Thus the heir to the heir is being initiated by an enabler
Of Britain's centuries-long killing sprees.

While all the time royalty profits from arms, due to its Crown Agents
Tending to its shares in Lockheed,
And nurturing bundles of the royal investments in BAE Systems –
In BAE's Depleted Uranium shells and landmines.

The latest landmines are designed to leap up out of the ground,
Triggered by children playing or walking nearby.
They'll detonate in mid-air and they'll sever limbs as bodies fall
While the shareholdings of the super-rich rise.

The Times has claimed the sovereign's wealth grows yearly by 20m
And in 2010 it announced the Queen "crowned a successful year
For her share portfolio, with a personal fortune totalling £290m"
Though elsewhere others have assessed it in billions.

Yet confronted by the true cost of UK weapons exported abroad,
Namely the Indonesian massacres in East Timor,
Her son Charles said, "If we don't sell arms to them, someone else will",
Blithely exposing the monarchy's moral vacuum –

A voracious vacuum that's unsatisfied by seven palaces
Which require over a thousand servants,
And security for the state's Holy Family, protected 24/7 by SAS patrols,
Is charged to the taxpayer without their permission.

After Prince Albert demanded tax money, known as the Civil List,
To fund himself "in the manner befitting a well-to-do gentleman" –
His descendants likewise insist that public funds
Fill their vacuums, oblivious to the country's economic black hole.

Thus Charles spends thirty thousand a year on a Highgrove florist,
And fifty thousand on train trips to spread his muddled message
Though he himself has more than sufficient from the Duchy of Cornwall Estates –
From its rack rents and its nonexistent social housing.

While royal security costs over fifty million a year,
Its total cost to the nation escapes scrutiny,
This being so that the "honour and dignity of the Crown" is upheld
And the monarchical mysteries lie undisturbed.

Tellingly, the state pantomimes from which royalty derives
So much of its symbolic impact
Requires processional horses drugged with acepromazine
So that they may be kept compliant throughout;

And the obedience required of royal servants
Is as abusive as their treatment of animals
With minor royals exercising the *droit de seigneur*:
Entering their quarters to treat them as sexual chattels.

Although this Civil List affords more than adequate provision
Royal acquisitiveness has to go one better:
Thus the Duchess of York is filmed accepting £30,000
In crisp notes from her supposed benefactor,

To whom she mentions that for a further £500,000 she'll provide
An introduction to her husband Prince Andrew,
Though, when confronted, royalty closes ranks and disdains
All such evidence of their naked, animal greed.

Prince Andrew's spoilt reaction to the scandal was to rail angrily
Against the Serious Fraud Office, his bête noir,
For their impudence in exposing bribery in Saudi arms deals
(From which he himself was a likely beneficiary).

At an official lunch in Kyrgyzstan, the Prince said petulantly
That those engaged in pursuing justice were "idiots"
Since, as the UK's trade envoy with responsibility for the arms trade,
He was sympathetic to bribery to secure contracts.

Then he attacked those who he claimed jeopardized a £43 billion deal
With Saudi Arabia for British arms
Berating their folly in spurning these "enhanced compliance processes"
Which in any case, said the Prince, should be legalized.

This connoisseur of depravity who makes a speciality
Of selling to brutal and undemocratic regimes
Achieves it by his bullying, cajoling and jeering at "idiots"
Those, in other words, obstructing the princely path.

"A famed vulgarian, his rudeness to the little people
Is equalled only by his fawning to the rich"
So wrote Nick Abbott, a London radio broadcaster,
As the prince's arrogance surfaced on Wikileaks —

Along with details of the Prince's extra-long ironing board
Which he insists on travelling with for his 'turnout'.
Queried, a flustered valet explained, "No one knows how to iron
His Royal Highness's trousers like me" —

Meanwhile Andrew's elder brother, the heir, dresses in eastern robes
And in curly-toed slippers to greet his guests —
A birthright sybarite whose footmen knelt to polish the bodywork,
Whitewashing the wheels of the royal baby's pram.

The un-Welsh Prince of Wales, Charles loses his temper
Whenever his staff's pampering falls below par:
If the gravel's not been swept, or shirts incorrectly folded,
Or clothes lie about wherever he's dropped them.

His socks must be daintily prepared so they're easy to put on
As hovering valets anxiously flit and fuss
Over his two thousand pound suits and thousand pound shoes
From Savile Row and Lobbs in St James's —

A niminy-piminy connoisseur of luxuriant products:
Of creams and unguents for royal primping;
A hedonistic perfectionist rumoured only to come to life
When berating staff for laying a crooked tablecloth;

Or when tearing a washbasin from a bathroom wall
And smashing it on the floor at Highgrove,
Because his monogrammed towels aren't replaced
Immediately after the prince has used them.

Originally the word 'aristos' in Greek would mean the best,
But later aristocracy just became an elitist pathology –
A mindset exemplified by Princess Anne on Christmas morning
When leaving Sandringham's Mary Magdalen church.

After she'd snatched a basket of flowers from a seventy-five year old lady
(Erroneously assuming they were intended for her),
The Princess was then told the old lady wished to hand them to the Queen Mother
At which Anne scoffed, "What a ridiculous thing to do."

This pensioner, who was engagingly called Mary Halfpenny,
Said "Princess Anne just grabbed it very roughly,"
Then Ms Halfpenny's friend, from Lincoln, Lesley Hirst, added:
"I think Princess Anne was exceedingly rude."

One of those later hearing the Princess snap at her nieces, "get a move on"
And preventing them taking flowers from well-wishers
Was reminded, as she watched the 'Princess Royal' stalking off,
That "pigs' ears are still not making silk purses".

Likewise when a colleague of Professor Dawkins was to challenge
The crank notions of Anne's sibling, Prince Charles,
Such as that crop circles are sent from elsewhere to homeopathically cure
Our inorganic world's disharmony,

Charles would pout and flush and then turn angrily on his heel
Leaving Richard Dawkins's colleague
To be berated by Charles's equerry tersely hissing,
"One does not argue with the Prince."

Besides commissioning a 'siege d'amour' (a chair that enabled his corpulent body
To be pleasured by more than one mistress at a time),
Queen Victoria's son Bertie would spend much of his Civil List cash
Trying to beat a record of 12,000 birds shot in a season;

And the royal passion for blood sports still rages, though none's a sport
Since the principal players are not asked permission
Before taking part in a game in which a deer learns it's lost
By being killed and decapitated; then stuffed and mounted.

Despite his shyness George VI was loath to allow a day
To pass without his taking a shot
And in 1924 he and his young wife, Elizabeth Bowes-Lyon,
Would go on a four-month African safari.

Elizabeth, later Queen and Queen Mother, had a Rigby rifle
And together they shot buffalo and waterbuck,
Then they shot antelope, Kenyan hartebeest and steinbuck,
Waterhog and jackal and rhinoceros.

In Uganda the future King George VI shot an elephant:
One with tusks weighing ninety pounds each.
"I was very lucky," the King said later, flushing with pride,
"As there are not very many big ones left."

Later George would introduce his eldest daughter
To the thrills of stalking and shooting stags.
The future Queen shot her first in 1945 aged sixteen
And Crawfie her governess recalled her excitement.

"We talked of nothing but stalking and antlers and points," Crawfie said.
"We had to retrace with her, in her mind,
Every exciting inch of the day. Then the stag's head was severed
For it to have pride of place at Balmoral."

By 1993 the Duke of Edinburgh, the owner of fifty-six shooting rifles,
Had brought down thirty thousand birds from the skies;
He'd killed two crocodiles, as well as scores of wild boar
Several hundred Scottish stags, and an Indian tiger.

The Duke of Edinburgh's accumulation of animal corpses,
Piled up over the past 40 years,
Ranges widely over continents, covering mammals and birds
For the tweedy Duke's jocular holocaust.

Figures compiled from press reports in Britain alone
Reveal this 'conservationist' as targeting hare,
Wild duck, snipe, woodcock, teal, pigeon and partridge –
Commandeering English wildlife with lead shot.

In 1993, at the Royal Family's Sandringham estate
Shooting pheasant daily, often with his wife,
The Duke hit a target of 10,000 during his seven-week stay
His Norfolk parties have now 'bagged' 150,000.

Should the Duke partially miss then a bird he's wounded
Is brought by a gundog to the royal group,
Where the Queen stands waiting with a convenient stick
And Her Majesty bludgeons it to death.

"Prince Philip especially enjoys shooting wild boar,
On the estates of friends in Germany.
On one occasion he and Prince Charles," wrote *The Independent*,
"Are said to have killed fifty wild boar in a single day."

Prince Philip frequently defends his love of blood sports
By claiming that he's 'culling', rather than killing
All the wildlife he's dispatching, though to wildlife itself
It's a distinction without a difference.

Alive to the importance of royal tradition, Prince Andrew
First took his daughter out shooting when she was six;
Perhaps the Prince told her all about 'culling' and 'killing'
Or perhaps he simply told her shooting was fun.

"Above all, he adores shooting rabbits," said a hunting friend
Of William's shooting in the hills above Loch Muick,
Though the trainee royal's late mother said she was sorry her sons
Were, in her words, "so keen on killing things".

To Diana they'd grown "into a couple of little thugs"
Who'd boast to classmates of "granny's castles" –
"When I'm king," Prince William would say when thwarted,
"I'm going to send my knights around to kill you."

"If you give me a hard time," he told a schoolboy opponent
"I'll get my dad to cut your head off."
As if aware of some entitlement to adopt the serial killer,
Henry the Eighth, as a murderous role model.

"They are never happier than when they have a gun in their hands."
Their mother noted, though warning them not to be photographed with guns,
"I told them," she said, "Remember, there is always someone in a high-rise flat
Who does not want you to shoot Bambis."

Unfazed, Harry's accused of shooting owl-like hen harriers
Of which there are only seven hundred breeding pairs –
The birds' offence being to compete with humans in taking grouse
Though the hen harrier only kills them to survive.

Equally undeterred, Harry's elder brother spots an Ibis –
A bird revered in ancient Egypt
As the envoy of Thoth, god of words and of wisdom,
When William is out hunting in Kenya.

This slow, graceful bird with a beak like a crescent moon
Is considered an omen but to William it's a trophy
And he opens both barrels though later, on learning it's endangered,
Says lamely, "I was told they were good enough to eat."

Royal killing sprees start young: Prince William would kill his first stag
On his grandmother's Birkhall estate, aged fourteen,
After which the head stalker, Sandy Masson, 'blooded' the boy
In an initiation rite that followed the royal slaughter.

Sadly, using a high-velocity rifle to size up a trophy stag
With the telescopic sights adjusted for him by a gillie
Doesn't quite match the mystique of plucking a sword from a stone,
So Merlin may have absented himself from this inaugural ritual.

He may also have withheld his magic when Charles took William
To Gloucestershire's Beaufort hunt and urged him to watch a kill –
For the English fox, as native to Merlin's soil as its ancient oaks,
May take precedence over Saxe-Coburg-Gothas.

"We must not let daylight in upon the magic," warned Walter Bagehot.
The Victorian was fearful people might see through it.
But Royalists still strive to extend his warning to the present
Though there's less magic in monarchy than ever.

For just as with Emperors and Czars, the 'magic' is manufactured:
Royal figures with a high profile due to saturation publicity
Are people pretending to be state symbols who often go mad,
In the same way zoo animals can die from being stared at.

Monarchy's like a stale Petri dish spawning celebrity clones
Who con the enfeebled into letting themselves be governed
By a vainglorious killer cabal endowed with whims of steel,
Whose history often shows them to be mad as hatters:

The present heir has famously said he wishes to be reincarnated
As one of his mistress's sanitary products;
His ancestor George III shook hands with a tree in Windsor Great Park
Thinking he was speaking to the King of Prussia;

Princess Alexandria of Bavaria said she'd swallowed a grand piano
As a child and believed this until she died;
King Ludwig II of Bavaria would swear day was night and night was day
Citing a moon he'd had painted on the ceiling as proof;

Prince Otto, his younger brother, decided that the only way
To keep his sanity while Ludwig was reigning
Was to shoot a peasant a day, so he shot them in the garden
Then would wonder why his garden was overgrown;

Catherine the Great locked up her hairdresser for over three years
To stop him spreading the news she had dandruff;
Prince Philip of Calabria was infatuated by pairs of gloves
Wearing up to sixteen pairs of silk ones at once;

King Charles VI of France was convinced he was made of glass
And he'd refuse to travel by carriage
In case the wheels' vibrations caused his body to shatter
Into millions of transparent splinters;

King Henry Christophe of Northern Haiti
Liked forcing his royal guards
To prove their loyalty by marching them off cliff-tops
While Henry executed those who refused;

Queen Juana of Spain went insane when her husband Philip died
And she wouldn't allow him to be buried;
But had his coffin accompany her wherever she travelled
Caressing his mummified flesh at mealtimes.

King Ferdinand II of Sicily would only allow his face
To be used on his mail service's postal stamps
On condition no franking mark was placed on his image
And all envelopes were handled with gloves;

As if inhabiting this same ballpark, the Queen refers to "dark forces
At work in this country, of which we know nothing" –
And similarly the doomed Diana thought, rightly or wrongly,
That assorted agents of darkness were trying to kill her:

"This particular phase in my life is the most dangerous –
My husband is planning 'an accident' in my car,
Brake failure and serious head injury in order," she'd write,
"To make the path clear for him to marry…"

As the royal brood mare she felt trapped, betrayed and maddened
Describing herself as a POW or Prisoner of Wales;
Disgusted by her loveless marriage she'd repeatedly throw up
Revolted by the husband who'd rejected her.

She produced an heir, as required, then a rumoured love-child
To restore her shattered self-esteem
Then she was tape-recorded, abused and rejected some more,
Whereupon she went off the rails, or was pushed.

Though her paranoia's unproven, rumour's wings can still flap
For those who rile the powerful, as she did, are at risk;
Thus Mike Mansfield QC points to Diana's crash as conveniently ending
Her opposition to the lucrative peddling of landmines.

But, from unending rumours of conspiracy with undemocratic forces
To the queen's being a twelve-foot lizard,
These fables reveal the mental imbalance of those force-fed
A remorseless diet of royal pap by an idle media.

Yet true or false, paranoid suspicions are a predictable byproduct
Of a plutocratic cult, still ring-fenced by force of arms –
A leftover from an Empire in which murder was a commonplace
But whose embers retain their powers of destruction...

Notably when Trinidad became a Dominion in 1962
A UK court was retained for its appeals,
Namely the Judicial Committee of the Privy Council,
And the Queen herself signs off the court's business.

Though Britain would shortly abolish capital punishment
Trinidad's government maintained the practice
And the anomaly meant that the Queen approved death warrants
Referred to her from this Judicial Committee.

Thus it's the case in the Caribbean, where Elizabeth is Queen:
In Belize; the Bahamas; Barbados; St Lucia and Jamaica;
And in St Vincent and the Grenadines; St Christopher and Nevis –
That a royal pen wields terminal power on Death Row.

Thus, as a direct result, on 16 May 1975 in Royal Gaol, Port of Spain,
The prison superintendent arrived at a cell door at dawn
And he handed Michael de Freitas, the prisoner waiting inside,
The dismissal of his last appeal, signed *'Elizabeth R'.*

Michael was hooded then led to the gallows under armed guard
And, while there's no death penalty in her own country,
Michael was hanged by the neck by royal command until Michael X,
Also known as Abdul Malik, was pronounced dead.

Years before, Michael had said that the monarchy would last longer
If Her Majesty were to have a black baby;
The British press were appalled, as they assumed his flip remark
Meant that Michael was offering his services as a stud.

On death row Michael fell to wondering if *"My cheekin' 'er caught me up"*
Then he'd say with a fatalistic grin,
"So now I'm in a cell in her <u>Royal</u> Gaol, and now it's her powerful <u>Royal</u> noose,
"That sends me to her <u>*Kingdom Come*</u>. Can you dig it?"

In his cage a light-bulb would burn throughout the night.
"We hear the flying of the trap," Michael told visitors;
And he'd indicate the death chamber just a few feet away,
Then he'd whisper, "We can hear it distinctly."

He'd also hear a Lord Kitchener calypso coming through
The Death Row radio's macabre crackle:
"When the judge accep' the verdict, he let the hammer bang.
Malik, he say nothing, But Queen say, 'One to hang.'"

For in the words of Lord Diplock, the senior presiding judge,
"Their Lordships will humbly advise Her Majesty
That the appeal should be dismissed..." His death warrant
Had been signed by the Queen on the 14th May, 1975

And when what the monarch had thinkingly, or unthinkingly, signed
Had been conveyed to the Governor General,
Michael would say to his wife, Désirée, "Better go home."
"This is no place for you, pretty girl."

In a manuscript smuggled out of Death Row Michael described
How on a Wednesday "the voices of all the prisoners
Would acquire a higher pitch" for those in the cells lived in dread
Of an impending message from the Governor General.

Each week Death Row's inhabitants were prepared for execution
Which fell on a Friday: "You are weighed," Michael wrote,
"The trap of the gallows is greased. All await that dreaded word,
'Greetings' if your time has arrived."

"Then – if it has – from the office at the far end of the corridor
"Come some officials, they'll stand in front of your cell
"And they'll salute you with this word from the Governor General:
"'Greetings.' Everyone waits for that terrible word.

"Most times hymns are sung. I pray. I hope someone, somewhere
Will listen, for in all Holy Books it is written
That justice should be tempered with mercy wherever possible."
But there was no mercy for Michael, just a white hood.

"If there is anyone in Trinidad who should get glory
For my coming, Abdul Malik is that person…"
Muhammad Ali had said of Michael X, who'd invited him
"To see the conditions his people were living in."

Then Allen Ginsberg wrote of "a new awareness that we were
All on the same boat of change"
And of being "armed to create Eden or Hell's fiery gardens
On our little ball rolling through the solar system".

Ginsberg added that Michael "was part of that communal effort
To work out our local destiny.
I pray with him that Mercy be the last judge of the world
And not our own cruel confused hearts.

"And in this context and the context of his karmic nobility
I here plead for his life. Om Ah Hum."
But with a pen-stroke the Queen showed she preferred Betjeman
To the poems of Allen Ginsberg or Muhammad Ali.

Kate Millett protested, "It's the hideous combination of racism
And sexism that permits these kind of trials to happen"
Predictably an appeal to the great-great-grand-daughter
Of Queen Victoria, legendary for her stiff-necked views

Such as "Women's rights are a mad, wicked folly" – were ignored,
And all pleas to Buckingham Palace went unanswered,
Indicating that the Head of the Anglican Church and the Defender of the Faith
Favours a more Old Testament view of religion.

Thus rather than Christ's revolutionary message of forgiveness
Her Governor's 'Greetings' brought revenge:
Michael was hanged, then drawn – meaning he was left to swing –
It being the Royal Gaol's colonial tradition.

In London those who felt British hypocrisy had overreached itself
Wrote Michael's name on the walls of Buckingham Palace:
'MICHAEL X', repeated six times, was followed by 'MICHAEL ABDUL MALIK'
But instead of an 'X' they added graveyard crosses.

On the 6th July 1999, twenty-five years after Michael's death
The same royal custom persists with nine executions in four days:
Trinidad's Prison Commissioner, Cipriani Baptiste, told the press
That the Royal Gaol's gallows had been freshly "oiled".

The condemned, Joel Ramsingh, Stephen Eversley and Bhagwandeen Singh,
Had once more been pricked by the royal Parker,
As had Dole Chadee; Joey Ramiah and Ramkhelawan Singh;
Clive Thomas; and Robin Gopaul and Russel Sankerali.

"No human life, no matter how wretched, is without worth,"
Said Sister Theresa DeAlva, a Catholic nun
Campaigning outside Royal Gaol against this mass execution,
"The men are still human beings, children of God."

The executions would take place despite appeals from Amnesty International
And from three Nobel Peace Prize winners, including Bishop Tutu;
It was as if the Parker pen's owner, always 'above politics', felt empowered
To strike through all pleas from the great and the good.

But given that it's Her Majesty's courts, Her Majesty's prison service,
Her Majesty's Inspectorate of Constabulary,
Her Majesty's Armed Forces; Her Majesty's government and taxes and subjects
Being quite so inordinately majestic could go to your head.

The well-worn pretence that the royal family's 'above politics'
And must therefore be beyond criticism,
Is constantly disproved, such as when the third in line to the throne
Directs US F15 jets to drop 500 lb bombs –

Prince Harry was sent to an Afghan warzone as political propaganda,
And with the complicity of a prostrate press
Who agreed to enforce a news blackout till the MoD had fully exploited him –
To glamorize their country's war and to attract recruits.

Harry's bombs land on an area of Afghanistan in February 2008,
And as 'Joint Terminal Attack Controller'
Harry slaughters 34 Afghanis by using what's nicknamed 'Kill TV'.
He's then thought to have boasted of it afterwards.

Codenamed 'Widow Six Seven' Harry studies a regional map.
He pokes a finger at where the enemy's likely to be,
Then he instructs US aircrews to blast 'Terry Taliban' to smithereens
As if Afghan tribespeople were merely Norfolk pheasants.

Again, if royalty was really above politics the Queen wouldn't ask
(As she did recently with a testy expression),
"Why" (she being so rich) *"no one foresaw the downturn in the economy...?"*
For it concerned her to be a fraction less wealthy.

Compare all this to the royal reaction to the Pan Am disaster at Lockerbie
When two hundred and fifty nine were killed –
It was described as "The largest mass murder on British soil"
And it was taken for granted the sovereign would visit.

But though the royal family happily use Scotland as its playground,
As a base from which to decimate its wildlife,
Their jammed moral compass insisted their schedule was full
And so regretfully they'd be giving Lockerbie a miss.

Although Edinburgh was Scotland's capital city,
Its Duke pleaded a prior engagement in Japan,
Then the Queen and Prince Charles also made their excuses
But it was agreed that Andrew might fit in an hour.

The exploding Boeing airliner had gouged out a crater
In Lockerbie's Sherwood Crescent
Killing eleven residents with the plane's falling parts
And injuring others with its impact explosions.

Andrew deigned briefly to appear at someone's bedside
Though only managing the dispiriting observation
That "This kind of thing was bound to happen sooner or later"
And adding, for no reason, "It's worse for the Americans."

Andrew's family may be sealed off within their billionaire bubbles
But such a studied reluctance to comfort the afflicted
Must inevitably tempt providence, if not the Greek Furies,
Always happiest when afflicting the comfortable.

"God save the Queen," the Sex Pistols spat venomously
"Our figurehead is not what she seems,"
"God save your mad parade," ran their incendiary song
"God save the queen; a fascist regime...!"

Edward VIII would visit Nazi Germany in 1937 to meet Adolf Hitler
And later he'd voice admiration for his policies –
The quondam King concluded, "It would be a tragic thing for the world
If [Adolf] Hitler were overthrown".

Following his elder brother's taking his honeymoon in the Third Reich
His successor, George VI, was also keen on appeasement:
And he even sent a royal escort to congratulate Chamberlain on his flight back
After his being deceived by Hitler at Munich.

Then when George VI thought the Empire was threatened by refugee Jews,
King George VI blithely said he was "glad to think
That steps are being taken to prevent these people
Leaving their country of origin."

Following George's concern, the King's Secretary, Halifax,
Was to telegraph the British Embassy in Berlin,
And Halifax asked them to encourage the German government
"To check the unauthorized emigration of Jews."

So when it came to anti-Semitism King George VI
May not have stuttered at all,
And even as late as 1970 his elder brother was telling interviewers:
"I never thought Hitler was such a bad chap."

Edward's cousin, Prince Philip, had four sisters married to Nazis
Yet was considered an eligible suitor for Princess Elizabeth
Despite his family, in Philip's own words, being "inhibited about the Jews"
And despite Philip's featuring at Nazi funerals.

In a family photograph Philip's youngest sister, Sophia,
Is seen opposite Hitler at Goering's wedding
Where every conceivable expression of racist excess
Would doubtless have been common currency.

Philip's brother-in-law, Prince Christophe von Hessen,
Served both in the SS and the Luftwaffe
He was even suspected of having bombed Buckingham Palace
In the hope of assassinating George and reinstating Edward.

In July 1940 while the exiled Edward was in Lisbon,
The German ambassador consorted with the former King
And then informed Berlin, "The Duke believes that continued heavy bombing
Would make England ready for peace."

Thus an embittered Edward was urging the bombing of his own people –
And with his wife (who'd had von Ribbentrop as a lover),
And with his aide, Fruity Metcalfe (a Mosley-ite Blackshirt),
They'd treacherously plot Edward's return as a Nazi puppet.

After the war, Edward's collusion proved embarrassing
And so the Queen's cousin, Sir Anthony Blunt,
An ex-Soviet spy, later in charge of the Queen's pictures,
Was asked to track down incriminating documents.

Blunt was sent to the Schloss Friedrichshof in Kronberg
To rescue Edward's Nazi correspondence –
Then, thanks to Blunt's helpfully concealing evidence of royal treason,
Blunt's own brand of treason was granted immunity.

Predictably, given his fascist flavouring, Philip's no stranger to genocide:
"In the event that I am reincarnated," Philip has said,
"I would like to return as a deadly virus" – thinking his high-handed cull
Would, in his words, "solve overpopulation,"

Such thoughts reflect a frequent hobbyhorse of the rich
Who morbidly dwell on threats from the poor.
Though the poor's footprint is minimal compared with their own
Yet the poor are targeted by plutocratic eugenicists.

Philip shares such eliminationist views with Henry Kissinger
The US war criminal (honoured by the Queen):
Kissinger says "depopulation should be the highest priority
Of U.S. foreign policy towards the Third World."

Predictably neither the Queen's Consort nor Kissinger
Propose to cull groups of arms dealers or militarists –
Their Fourth Reich of the über-rich has it in for the Third World
While plutocrats are encouraged to breed as they please.

"He's bad tempered, ill-educated and probably won't be faithful,"
Was reputedly the verdict of George VI
On Prince Philip whom George VI's wife would refer to
As 'the Hun', singling him out for especial loathing.

Prince Philip, who was at first known as Battenberg,
Later anglicized to Mountbatten,
In fact shared the original name Schleswig-Holstein-Sonderberg-Glucksberg-Beck
After the family's alma mater, a Prussian principality.

But on advice, this mouthful was downsized to the name 'Windsor'
Lifted from an English town and an English family —
A ruse to deflect prejudice against intrusive Prussian princelings
With their passion for large families and dead animals.

Yet their anglicizing an irksome past proves only a cosmetic ploy —
As in the case of Princess Michael of Kent, formerly Reibnitz —
An SS officer's daughter who was heard bawling at African Americans
In a New York restaurant, *"You need to go back to the colonies."*

Likewise the Queen's sister Princess Margaret (who was so royal
That she'd sometimes answer the 'phone
With the matchless phrase, "This is royalty speaking"
As if expecting a long-distance curtsey)

Walked out of the film *Schindler's List* in a huff
Because she thought it was "anti-German".
It was "a tedious film about Jews", she told her butler
And strongly advised him to give it a miss.

The Princess's views on any races or condition of men
That differed from her own were distasteful:
She told Chicago's mayor the Irish were "pigs, all pigs"
And as for India, she hated "those little brown people".

Despite Margaret's being the patron of a children's charity
For the mentally handicapped –
The Princess rounded on one of its units' staff, saying
"I don't want to meet any daft children."

Princess Margaret would parrot the views of the Queen Mother,
An unabashed supporter of white rule;
When granddaughter Margaret referred to the Rhodesian majority
As either "blackamoors" or else "nig nogs".

At the time it was thought the Pistols' accusations of fascism
Were outrageous, and totally off target
Yet fascism, defined as corporate elitism plus violence,
Can shape-shift and adopt user-friendly disguises.

"Prince Charles," ran a headline, "was last night accused
Of driving his tenant farmers towards suicide
With a £2.3 million pound rent demand as foot-and-mouth
Swept his Duchy of Cornwall estate."

A corporate empire of 240 farms gives him a vast income
Of over four million pounds a year –
His feudal rents are due for payment on Lady Day, March 29th
And then again on Michaelmas, September 29th.

Recently this particular income has shot up by eleven per cent
Thus transforming the Prince's tenants into near-serfs –
With his Duchy management charging rack rents for village halls
Which the Duchy threatens to demolish if the locals can't pay.

Prince Charles was warned at the height of the foot and mouth epidemic
That the exorbitant rents which he was charging
For wide-ranging swathes of his unearned landholdings
Were in danger of driving tenants to despair.

Noel Cartwright, of South West Tenant Farmers' Association
Spelled it out in clear terms for Charles' benefit:
"The risk of suicide among farmers is a major worry
This could push our members over the edge."

But there are none so deaf as those who won't listen
(Albeit that some are born with capacious ears) –
Farmers lost their stock but it was still business as usual
For the Duchy of Cornwall's organic cupidity.

With two farmers a week committing suicide in the rural crisis,
Publicly, the Prince wrung his hands in anguish –
Though his tenants were quick to distrust his crocodile tears,
"The Duchy is sympathetic as long as you pay the rent."

With a low-minded cunning the Duchy's land agents are all on contracts
Each one of which is performance-related –
So Prince Charles' rent collectors are given a financial incentive
To see the money in Charles' bank account on time.

In other words, royal money-grubbing is built into the system
And should tenants be unable to furnish their landlord
With the funds to pay his servants to squeeze out his toothpaste,
Then both they and their families face cruel eviction:

Shovelled off into a caravan or a windy tent in a hedgerow
Upon the signature of this spendthrift heir to the throne,
With his three chauffeurs; twenty-five butlers; dressers and chefs
And his white leather lavatory-seat for travelling.

When the head of the family or, as the Duke calls it, 'the Firm',
Describes shooting as "an intelligent leisure activity" for a child;
Or when his grandson, Prince William, inspecting Trident submarine crews,
Applauds those carrying nuclear payloads as "heroes",

Then the Royal Family's dominant message can be decoded
As the defence of the Firm's assets through armed force,
Rather than to love your neighbour in communities free of division
Or to set examples of fair dealing and goodwill.

Long-suffering retainers of such 'royals' are paid pitifully
Then abandoned when they're of no use
Or when they flout royal etiquette, as did the Queen's Nanny Crawfie
Who'd unwisely describe life in the royal nursery.

Nanny Crawfie disclosed the fact that Her Majesty
Had an Obsessive Compulsive Disorder
And had to arrange all her clothes in a special order.
Crawfie was dropped from their Christmas list and cast out.

Year after year old retainers have waited by windows
Hoping their former employers would visit
And each Christmas, Nanny Crawfie waited expectantly
As her Queen swept past her en route to Balmoral.

Likewise the Queen's scandalous neglect of her first cousins,
Katherine and Nerissa Bowes-Lyon,
Who were subnormal and left to rot in a Scottish asylum
And then given a paupers' funeral.

Royal Christmases celebrate both killing and consumption:
By shooting birds and continuous meals –
For all their nods to the memory of an ascetic Jewish pacifist
And the platitudes commemorating his birth.

Lunch is over when the head of the Church,
Her Majesty, the Monarch, proclaims:
That *'It's nearly three. Time to watch **me** on TV'*
And then all adjourn for her broadcast,

During which bland Christmas clichés are trotted out
With a hefty nod to Britain's profitable war machine:
Though Christian peace should require them to be dismantled
The Queen's armed services are sanctimoniously blessed.

The royal family dutifully watch their matriarch
While they anticipate the Boxing Day shoot.
Some bet on whom amongst them will shoot the most birds –
The most number of nature's freest spirits.

Christmas paper crowns are worn by killing machines:
As Lennon sang, "There's room at the top...
But first you must learn how to smile as you kill,
If you want to be like the folks on the hill."

And the folks on the hill are rich beyond avarice
And they give their consent to any war going:
Illegal, dishonest wars fought for ignominious profit –
No royal figurehead ever says its wars are a lie.

Instead the 'Firm' is overindulged with media oxygen
Leading to the looniest distortions of common sense
In which, for example, one in ten primary school children in 2010
Believed the Queen had invented the telephone.

"The Sovereign can do no wrong and no laws can be brought against her."
According to Lord Halsbury in *The Laws of England*
But a democratic monarchy is an oxymoron, and as regards transparency
The royal drawbridge is invariably pulled up –

While royal trivia gets saturation coverage: in April 2011
The BBC's lead story was the fact that William
"Won't wear a ring. His father does, but his grandfather doesn't"
This royal fetishism is passed off as news.

In the US, 74 people earn the same as the bottom 19 million
Thanks to which their society makes no sense;
And royalty too bears this same economic mark of Cain
It makes claims on society through its irrelevant wealth –

The royals run a Wonderland caucus race where the ignoble get prizes:
Such as a knighthood, for example, for Norman Schwarzkopf,
The US general, who said Iraq's dead "weren't worth counting"
And another knighthood for Kissinger, a war criminal –

Who swaggeringly proclaimed power was an aphrodisiac
After he'd carpet-bombed Cambodia.
"Why should we flagellate ourselves" the dissembling Sir Henry likes to ask,
"For what the Cambodians did to each other?"

"I want every Iraqi soldier bleeding from every orifice."
General Schwarzkopf would sadistically announce
After which the Queen gave this ghoul her greatest honour
Following his genocidal bloodletting in US wars.

Other pillars of the American state join in the queue for rewards –
Royalty-mongering spectres of the US machine:
Caspar Weinberger, of the Iran-Contra drugs for arms affair,
And Brent Scowcroft, Kissinger's gofer, are Knights of the British Empire.

"For services to law enforcement" J. Edgar Hoover, the head of the FBI,
Who had half of the Black Panther party murdered,
And who phone-tapped Martin Luther King for over ten years
Is pleased to find himself similarly ennobled.

As is Alan Greenspan, the financier who endorsed toxic derivatives
To create a housing bubble making the rich even richer;
An economic war criminal who fetishized market forces –
Sir Alan is now a Knight of the British Empire.

The fact that each US President's record, without exception,
Would earn them seats in the dock at Nuremburg
Or at the International Criminal Court on genocide charges
Doesn't deter the Royal Family from honouring them.

For by an ironic twist each US President morphs into George III
Against whom their forbears fought:
They declare war on a whim, they're tyrannical plutocrats
And they imprison their own people without trial.

The US has been infatuated with the monarchist mindset
From the US republic's very earliest days:
A crawling John Adams proposed they give their first President
The fatuous title of "His Exalted High Mightiness".

So two Presidents are made knights of the Queen's crooked table:
George H.W. Bush senior and Ronald Reagan –
Both guilty of war crimes in Nicaragua and El Salvador
And misguidedly bombing Iraq and then Libya.

Next comes Colin Powell who presented some talcum powder to the UN
Claiming it was anthrax and thus a pretext for war:
Sir Colin is made a knight – the man who covered up the My Lai massacre –
The man who torched Vietnamese villages with his Zippo lighter.

"We burned down the thatched huts," Powell confessed,
"Starting the blaze with Ronson and Zippo lighters.
Why were we torching houses and destroying crops?
Ho Chi Minh had said his 'people were like the sea

In which guerrillas swam'. ... We tried to solve the problem
By making the whole sea uninhabitable.
In the hard logic of war, what difference did it make if you shot
Your enemy or starved him to death?"

Sir Colin Powell, supervisor of turkey shoots as Iraqi soldiers
Tried to retreat from Basra and were fried,
Betrayed Dr King's nonviolence, preferring the craven acceptance
Of a bauble from Great Britain's Queen.

Another royal investiture was held for the US General Tommy Franks
Who oversaw the looting of hospitals in Baghdad
And whose forces thought it fun to fire on Iraqi ambulances –
Sir Tommy now joins these sorry knights of a twisted table –

Where Kissinger is a 'Knight Commander of the Most Distinguished Order
Of St. Michael and of St. George',
Though Sir Henry is neither angelic nor has he killed any dragons
But has only napalmed poor peasant farmers in fields.

And should anyone be inclined to study Kissinger's nobility any further,
He is so inured to genocide that he once advised Nixon,
"If they put Jews into gas chambers in the Soviet Union
It is not an American concern."

Yet they're singled out by the Crown for aggrandizement
These characters who've remained unchanged
Since the time of the Roman historian, Tacitus, who said,
"They plunder, they slaughter, and they steal:

"This they falsely name Empire," Tacitus wrote on Rome's expansionist wars,
Adding, "and where they make a wasteland,
They call it peace." His verdict is just as applicable
To creatures from this same swamp millennia later.

George V would even make knighthoods dictator-friendly
By his bestowing one on Italy's Mussolini;
Then 'Bomber' Harris, Dresden's terror-bomber, received the same honour –
A serial war criminal by his own admission.

Shimon Peres, the ethnic cleanser of Palestine's West Bank
Who installed nuclear weapons at Dimona,
And who ordered the Qana massacre of children in Lebanon –
Sir Shimon is made another Knight of St George.

But when monarchs give out their decorations to unashamed murderers
To whom no crime against humanity is too gross,
A child might ask (as one did at a similar ceremony),
'Mummy, what are those people for?'

If you're royal, England's virtually your private estate
From where, after swanning about in stately homes,
You emerge to wave waves to the general population,
Then to hand out titles and tin medals to your estate workers –

To those who gather in your country's cultural harvest,
Not forgetting to reward your military back-up:
All those risking their lives for Britain's corporate plantations
Where its minerals and oil wealth are to be found.

The monarchy's acquisitive politics are revealed in Andrew's citation
When bestowing a U.S. Navy Captain, John Peterson,
With an 'Honorary Order of the British Empire' for leading joint forces
In the campaign to secure Iraqi oil assets.

For Britain's military a special order was created by George 1st
Derived from the medieval custom of bathing a knight –
Though sadly the recipients of this 'Most Honorable Order of the Bath'
Would be more noted for bloodbaths than for any that cleanse.

But beneath such ceremonial flummery lies an institutional cruelty:
Take racing, where four hundred horses are annually shot for the Queen's hobby;
Or polo, where cuts on ponies' flanks show how obedience is obtained
For princely players wearing harsh metal spurs.

This life-threatening family lives in a Palace posted with Life Guards
Wearing head-dresses coming from lifeless black bears
Hunted especially in Canada, shot and skinned for the fur hats
Which royal guards wear in sentry boxes while saving their Queen.

She's also saved by Tories who see monarchy as a confirmation
Of the Tory's presumptive right to rule
So they mythologize the institution; they mount it on a pedestal
And they grant the boss class's godhead whatever it chooses.

Thus despite three million unemployed and cuts in social spending
Prime Minister Cameron declares the royal wedding exempt:
It rebrands the royal franchise and it's the Tories' lucky wishbone
And so no wedding expense should be spared.

When the royal engagement is announced at a cabinet meeting
Cameron encourages his colleagues to bang the table
And to rejoice in an unrestrained worship of wealth and privilege
In "a sort of weird aristocratic fertility rite".

Labour has been equally craven since Ramsay MacDonald
Turned up at the Palace wearing top hat and tails,
Likewise Labour's former leader, Ed Miliband, denounces the Transport Union
For proposing strike action during William's wedding —

Royal spin doctors try to brand the wedding a 'people's wedding'
On the feeble grounds they'll be having limos as well as carriages
But the democratic deficit will be obvious to all those watching:
As royal etiquette still insists they're 'subjects' not citizens —

With the result that a democratically elected head of state
Is 'granted' a weekly audience with the Queen
From which, when it's over, he must walk out backwards —
It being disrespectful to turn your back on the monarch.

And royalty's dealings are automatically excluded
From the Freedom of Information Act
By which statute it's made clear that the interests of royalty,
Are more important than those of mere people.

As if inhabiting another world, at the royal stag party,
Both brothers plan with their Norfolk chums
To squeeze triggers on yet another slaughter of the innocent
Thus reminding William's bride she's marrying death.

It's organized by Harry, a party animal with a temper
Whenever the royal right to fun is threatened —
As when a manager, Francois Ortet, banned him from his Wiltshire bar:
Ortet was rounded on as a "fucking frog."

To Harry, Arabs are 'rag heads' and Pakistanis are 'pakis';
A favourite waterhole is a Soho sex club called 'The Box'
Where clients pay a thousand pounds for a table
To watch an acrobatic burlesque –

Which is overseen by a half-naked MC called 'Raven O'
Whose hair's fashioned into devil horns
And who squawks, "Do all the drugs you want. Do all the cocaine you can.
Answer every fetish. Drugs are good."

While a performer simulates inhaling drugs
"Off the stomach of a scantily-clad female"
And a naked man puts on a pig mask that's set alight
By two women in a sado-masochist ritual.

Then another woman – known only as "Laqueefa",
According to an *Evening Standard* snoop
Somehow manages to "play the tune of a popular song
Just by manipulating her genitalia."

Then when the Prince is sated he stumbles out slack-jawed
Signalling a royal limo to sweep out of the shadows
And dutifully drive a racist debauchee to a choice of palatial pad
While he brays incoherently of his conquests.

Later wedding invitations are dispatched from Clarence House
And it's confirmed that the King of Bahrain
Will be an honoured guest of the British royal family –
A man who tortures human rights activists;

A man who describes them as Bahrain's "terrorists"
Despite he himself ordering a massacre of five hundred people
In Pearl Square in the middle of Manama, Bahrain's capital –
Just a week before his invitation is sent out.

But since the King's son maintains a suite in the Dorchester,
And since he was also a pupil at Sandhurst;
And since his father, King Hamad, buys weapons from Britain
With which to murder civilian protestors;

And since the King is Patron of the Sandhurst Foundation;
And since he gave Prince Charles an Aston Martin
And since he guards his privileges with UK crowd-control weapons…
The King's personal conduct is judged irrelevant.

The Kings of Jordan, and Saudi Arabia, and Malaysia
Are also invited to the wedding –
A smorgasbord of royal pathology of whom the most fawned on
By his fellow royals is simply he who's the richest.

This is King Abdullah, a man who orders decapitations
In Riyadh's 'Chop Chop Square'
Amputates hands; flogs for deviance and drunkenness
And whose sentences can be spun out for months.

As for the bride she's being prepared by eating *foie gras* in Knightsbridge;
She lunches with Camilla to discuss wedding plans –
They consume geese forcibly stuffed to swell their livers and to delight gourmets
While they discuss a wedding that stiffs the public for twenty million

Despite their own country suffering from swingeing government cuts
While the royals gain millions in added funding,
Due to a Parliamentary device called a 'sovereign support grant',
Giving them fifteen percent more of Crown Estate profits.

This ploy gleans another forty million a year from Crown properties
And increases Royalty's income from its land holdings
Though all of this acreage has been of dubious title since 1649
When the Diggers declared it "a common treasure house to all".

To the revolutionary John Milton, "The trappings of a monarchy
Would set up an ordinary commonwealth."
And Shelley scorned monarchy as "the string that holds a robber's bundle".
He might have added 'that strangles its subjects' –

For, sat like a fat fairy on top of the arms trade's Christmas tree,
It cynically profits from war's being 'the health of the state'
And it has done so with royal approval of a million dying in Iraq,
For war's a royal hobby, just as is killing animals for sport,

Though to let your own subjects be sacrificed to an illegal war
To allow them to be gulled by 'Queen and Country';
To have hundreds of your subjects dying for a foreign Empire
Would not long ago have amounted to treason.

Charles 1st would be tried for having secretly treated
With a hostile power, namely Spain;
So a monarchy that's been prostituted by the US Empire
Has put itself in just the same position.

For all its heritage bling and its armed ceremonial
It conceals a squalid capitulation
Whereby England becomes a Disneyfied landing strip
Somewhere to the right of Washington.

"There's people at this moment", warned the band Crass
In a telling song 'The Gasman Cometh'
"There's fingers on the trigger. There's loyalty and royalty
To make their violence figure".

"Get well soon", says Charles stiltedly to a half- incinerated soldier
And the war veteran replies, "Yes sir, I will",
And this tragic farce continues with lip service to "our brave lads" –
The victims of a monarchy's class relations –

And of politicians' sloganeering, "Support the troops"
When they really mean 'Support arms industry profits' –
A deadly doublespeak that serves to persuade young lives
Of an inglorious duty to end up as state compost.

Lives are even shed to enrich a royal arms dealer
Around whom grotesque headlines whirl:
"Prince Andrew and the 17-year-old girl his sex offender friend," scream the tabloids,
"Jeffrey Epstein, flew to Britain to meet him".

Troops die "for British values" and taxpayers are impoverished
So that the fourth in line to the throne,
A self-styled "prince of the blood" can stay in Manhattan
With a paedophile called Jeffrey Epstein.

Andrew is "guarded by the Royal protection squad"
While young girls are sexually exploited
"By Epstein's adult male peers," who make free with them
Including, as the paper alleges, "royalty".

Yet when Andrew's suitability for public office
Is questioned in the House of Commons
By Labour's justice spokesman, adding he was also troubled
By the Prince being such a "very close friend"

Of Saif Gaddafi, the son of the Libyan dictator
And of a gun smuggler, Karuk Taituni,
He's officiously warned by the Speaker that his references
To royalty be "Very rare, very sparing and very respectful."

Both the Premier and the Palace's spin-doctors insist
That the Duke's contributions are "invaluable"
And figures for his weapons' sales are impressively massaged
(In the hope that his other massages go away).

Then, breathtakingly, as if to emphasize how impervious
Royalty can be to all popular feeling,
Prince Andrew is awarded the highest possible honour
For his 'personal service' to the Queen.

Despite a "continuing row over his close friendships
With a convicted paedophile and tyrannical foreign regimes,"
The Duke of York, the royal gunrunner for UK PLC, is driven to Windsor
For his proud mother, the Queen, to invest him.

The Queen makes him a Knight Grand Cross of the Royal Victorian Order,
The highest honour in the monarch's gift to bestow.
She personally decides to accord him the insignia's highest rank
After which the two royals, mother and son, "take tea".

With Her Majesty benefiting from her investments in munitions
It must have been easy to reward an arms-dealing son,
Though harder to reconcile with also being head of a church
Founded by a Middle Eastern anarcho-pacifist.

When Christ said 'suffer the little children to come unto me,'
He made no mention of wishing them slaughtered
By child-unfriendly bombs made by Royal Ordnance
Nor by the deadly toys of Britain's BAE systems, royally blessed –

Nor does the Bible permit the head of the Anglican church
To rewrite the New Testament's Beatitudes
So that divine dispensation may be granted to British tank shells
Allowing them to be tipped with Depleted Uranium.

But despite the Queen's GCVO, the Prince still remained
An excruciating "national embarrassment"
And an old friend of Andrew's would disloyally reveal,
"There appears to be no discernible mental activity."

It's almost as if he's been bred for an unthinking role
In serving the royals' imperial interests
And the family's lack of reflection never ceases to surprise
Given the extent of the monarchy's crimes:

Crimes that outweigh those of the tin-pot dictators
To whom the oafish Andrew is trying to sell arms
In exchange for golf trips and free junkets in Thailand
And a thousand royal servants at his beck and call.

Behind every great fortune there lurks a great crime
And this particular monarch is the beneficiary
Of dividends produced by an empire's corpse mountain –
Vast sums squirrelled away without apology.

It began with the Royal namesake Elizabeth I licensing thieves
And kitting them out as predatory pirates
For the purpose of raiding Spanish ships, then plundering their contents,
And bringing stolen gold to their pimping 'Gloriana'.

Thus as Britain became rich it wished to expand,
Using any pretext or deception to do so,
Such as declaring Ireland to be 'a barren wilderness'
So its inhabitants could be swept aside.

As a result royal favourites would receive tracts of land
As plantations for Britain's cash crops
With the language and rights of the local population
Suppressed and killed off by the crown.

In Ireland Dublin's Dean Swift was prompted to despair
That, "One-half of all Irish rents is spent in England
"And is squeezed out of the blood and vitals of Irish tenants,
"Who all live worse than any English beggar."

As Britain increased its appetite for luxuries further
It would extend its foreign possessions
Then, being genteelly disdainful of dirtying its hands,
It industrialized slavery as a solution.

The defenseless and vulnerable were hunted down
And rounded up by bribery and terror;
Sold on to the middlemen who traded in forced labour
To produce the Empire's new necessities.

Royal palaces paid for with slavery's products: sugar, tobacco, rubber and tea,
Were built by England's own indentured labourers;
'King Emperors' would then fill the palaces, with the acolytes they'd ennobled
And all demanding to be treated like gods.

The dark side of the British Empire grew murkier still
Thanks to its late Victorian holocausts:
In which thirty million died through the engineered famines
That lasted twenty years in the Indian subcontinent –

Due to the Empire's use of state-backed forced labour;
A further four million died in Bengal's famine,
Thanks to a meanness that was built into Imperial policy:
Of refusing food to a "feckless poor who'd breed".

A free-market ideology mixed with colonial callousness
Would lead to serial mega-deaths;
There were thousands more victims in Malaya and Africa
In British-owned mines and plantations –

Men, women and children had their lives cut short,
Killed or maimed in the lengthy construction
Of the imperial railways for transporting produce
Under the armed protection of imperial troops.

The concentration camp was a British invention
Under Queen Victoria in the Boer War;
And in her Indian camps Her Majesty's officers
Would conduct proto-Nazi experiments –

They were to see how few calories Indian coolies needed
And still be able to perform hard labor;
Such camp's rations were less than in Buchenwald,
Something Imperial apologists forget.

They forget too that their adored icons such as Churchill
Urged Britain to have its Empire 'on the cheap'
Through using aerial bombing, machine guns and poison gas
To suppress rebellions and unwelcome protest.

"I do not understand this squeamishness", Churchill declared,
"About the use of gas"
And elsewhere he'd repeat, "I am strongly in favour
Of using poisoned gas against uncivilized tribes."

Thus poison gas was used on Iraq in the 1920s
Simply to secure oil for the British Navy,
And Sudanese villages were trashed after World War One
For objecting to Britain's control of the Nile.

In India and the Middle East every extreme method was used
Merely to resolve labour disputes,
Or brutally to punish the non-payment of taxes to Britain
During Gandhi's non-violent resistance.

In the 1920s and early thirties Mohandas Gandhi
Was enemy No. 1 to Britain's King Emperor
Who Churchill advised "will, sooner or later,
Have to be grappled with and finally crushed."

"It is alarming and also nauseating to see Mr Gandhi"
Churchill magniloquently announced,
"A seditious middle temple lawyer, now posing
As a fakir of a type well known in the east,

"Striding half-naked up the steps of the vice-regal palace,
While he is still organizing and conducting
A defiant campaign of civil disobedience, to parley on equal terms
With the representative of the King-Emperor."

Although the Mahatma was the equal of any King-Emperor
His advice was ignored and instead Battenberg, aka Mountbatten,
Prince Philip's uncle, invigilated Indian partition so hurriedly
That it resulted in a million deaths and is still causing more.

Then in pursuit of its post-colonial economic goals
Britain has had direct responsibility
For suppressing independence movements in Indonesia
And for the bombing of Yugoslavia;

For invading Iraq (yet again), for bombing Afghanistan (yet again);
For waging war in Yemen, Egypt and Iran;
For supporting state killings in apartheid South Africa
And for backing the invasion of East Timor.

For having funded General Pinochet's coup in Chile;
And for Great Britain's so-called 'left', its pink Tories,
Arming the Nigerians in their war against Biafra,
Solely to protect corporate oil.

Worse still, counter-insurgency troops
Left England for South East Asia
And covertly supported US crimes in Vietnam,
Blessed by royal colonels-in-chief.

They then returned with a 'South Vietnam' bar
Attached to their General Service medal
Though their government was dishonestly denying
British troops were ever involved.

Yet thus, and most shabbily, and with the royal imprimatur
UK lives were sacrificed to American aims –
To the US's Vietnam holocaust with its four million dead.
The UK monarch fuelled a fascist Empire in Asia.

And however you cut it the sovereign was commander-in-chief
Of British army death squads roaming Ireland,
Killing Catholics in collusion with the Ulster Constabulary,
And killing them with total impunity.

Thus if you factor in the suppression of Mau Mau
And the castration of the Kenyan landless;
Plus the Aden killings of the 1960s, and massacres
Of communist insurgents by the Scots Guards...

If you factor in the decapitation of so-called bandits
By Royal Marine Commandos in Perak,
And the bombing of Malaya during the so-called 'Emergency' –
Four centuries of this yields a bodycount of millions,

While the benefit from such imperialist corpse-making
Has been enriching royal bank accounts –
It's added multiple zeros to royal names, or to their nominees,
At Coutts bank, or at Rothschilds, or at Barings.

In exchange royalty swans past, waving with lofty serenity
While it pretends that none of this happened –
It promotes its trite fables while covering up financial gain
Never apologizing for its investments' side effects...

During the Raj, in the Punjab city of Amritsar,
Britain's local Panjandrum
A Brigadier General Reginald Dyer issued two orders:
One ordered all the Indians using the main street

To crawl its entire length on their hands and knees,
And the other authorized a public whipping
For citizens of Amritsar who should find themselves
Within a *lathi* length of a British policeman.

A protesting crowd gathered in Jallianwallah Bagh,
Amritsar's park, on April 13, 1919
Where they listened to the testimony of victims
All of them unarmed and peaceable.

Dyer appeared at the head of a large contingent
Of British troops then, without warning,
He ordered his machine gunners to open fire.
They pierced two and three bodies at a time.

The shooting continued for a quarter of an hour
Until the ammunition ran out;
It killed three hundred and seventy nine people,
All of them huddling together in fear.

During Indian royal tours monarchs have been invited
By relatives of Amritsar's victims to say sorry,
But each time the sovereign's advisers have huffily told them
That apologies aren't what monarchy does best.

Though eventually, in 1997, by arrangement with the Foreign Office
In an attempt to rebrand the empire as benign
Both Her Majesty the Queen and the Duke of Edinburgh,
Were persuaded to visit Amritsar's Monument.

There they would read on its commemorative plaque
"This place is saturated with the blood
Of about two thousand Hindus, Sikhs and Muslims
Who were martyred in a non-violent struggle."

The Duke, however, harrumphed with indignation
And turned on his heel as he said,
"That's a bit exaggerated, it must include the wounded"
And he implied it was beneath his notice.

Royalty is now a dusty cherry on an imperial cake,
Left stranded as the Empire's receded –
Superfluous to requirements and, so stale and tasteless,
An heir once let slip, "I don't want to be King."

Yet it persists like an unlanced boil in the body politic –
A musty legacy of accumulated atrocities
Ever cognizant of the sinister advice of James 1st's Chancellor,
"Democracy is the deadliest enemy to a monarchy"

But while the UK's fake democracy shells out a hundred million,
Year in and year out for royalty's upkeep,
Michael Fagan who once broke into the Queen's bedroom
Is celebrated in subversive songs as a hero;

And it's significant that Iceland, Bermuda, Puerto Rico and others are happy
Not only without an indulgent royal family
But they also manage without having armed forces at all
No armies, nor any monarchs to extol violence.

Sir Henry Kissinger, knighted by the Queen, has said,
"Military men are dumb stupid animals
To be used as pawns for foreign policy," and, like dutiful puppets,
The Queen's soldiers are fed into US infernos.

The United States of Profiteers from Perpetual Wars is an ally
And whenever any of its plutocratic presidents
Yells out for cannon fodder for any of its imperial ventures
Little Britain subjects its citizens to the US's death wish.

Two million would protest against Iraq's gang-rape
Yet it made not the slightest difference
Just as if serving Queen and Country and the US Empire
Was some preordained destiny like Kismet.

I once watched the broadcast of Princess Anne's wedding
With a child aged eight, my daughter;
She looked away from the screen then she asked, "Why?
Why's she a Princess, Dad?"

Glancing at the laborious ceremony I tried to explain
Then gave up, "Oh, it's just nonsense –
Tosh made up for the tourists", "But Dad," she persisted,
"She's all dressed up like a Princess.

"And they're treating her as if she's a real Princess.
Look at all of them carrying her dress.
So, can she tell if there's a pea under a mattress?
Like Princesses can in fairy books?"

"Well, no, she can't do that, I'm afraid," I replied –
Sad that she should feel let down; she then paused,
"So she's not a Princess then Dad, is she? It's crap."
Then she got up and turned the television off.

Looking back, such a response was a survival tactic,
For why would a growing child nowadays need
To weaken its immune system with notions of deference
Or be blackmailed into thinking class was magic.

For the monarchy to become catnip to tourists (and terrorists),
A superstition is carefully orchestrated –
Using canapés at the Palace; silly medals and Mad Star Disease –
Props and stage sets to make the state irresistible.

Though for a young mind to be made susceptible
To this hereditary trick by fossilized spivs
Has to be an unhelpful learning experience
As it's guaranteed so repeatedly to go wrong:

"I don't dislike babies, though I think very young ones
Rather disgusting," Queen Victoria said,
Despite imposing her multiple offspring on the country,
Offspring who make England's finest spirits throw up.

The shades of Wat Tyler, of John Ball, Jack Cade and William Morris;
Of William Blake and of Thomas Paine;
Of Mary Wollstonecraft, and Shelley and Gerard Winstanley,
Have to gag daily at monarchy's repugnance.

How far kingship's declined in a child's eyes can be gathered
From Richard the Lion Heart in Robin Hood's time:
Who, whether true or false, stood for "a just and fair England" –
A far cry from cold landlords and creepy profiteers.

A far cry from the current reincarnations of King John,
With his Sheriff's hands in the till —
From the tormentors of bears, birds and wild boar;
From fox-hunters slashing horses and shooting stags;

From abattoir attendants dressing up their warfare state in military tat;
From grisly accumulators of diamonds and gold and weapons;
From judicial killers whose bejewelled fingers sign death warrants
Without a second thought of the consequences.

"I never wonder to see men wicked", said Jonathan Swift,
"But I often wonder to see them not ashamed."
Yet thanks to the wonder of Hanoverian haughtiness the word "sorry"
Loses its way before finding the royal lips.

"This other Eden", Shakespeare wrote in Richard II,
This "demi-paradise, this happy breed of men,
This little world, this precious stone set in the silver sea,
This blessed plot, this earth, this England."

Shakespeare would now see a monarchy empty of atmosphere
With its magnetic pole shifted elsewhere:
A royalty changed to heritage showbiz for the dull-witted
Peddling packets of crested Duchy biscuits —

While hiding haughty tycoons and bloodthirsty dullards
Who take out their sorry inadequacies
On creatures they judge to be their inferiors, if not vermin,
While they themselves live off the labour of centuries.

To the Queen's advisers she must seem the ultimate insider trader
As, thanks to her Red Boxes, she's ahead of the game –
Having advance knowledge of any country's ups and downs –
Useful, as in racing, to those buying and selling.

On the Queen's accession it was said she was worth 300 million –
Now the royal nest egg's said to be 17 billion.
Her investments in BP and in Rio Tinto Zinc mean, very simply,
She profits from petrol and uranium, and her subjects get ill.

After the Queen had been the first person to switch on nuclear power,
At Calder Hall in Cumbria in the nineteen-fifties,
The world's first nuclear power station was followed by Sizewell B,
And the Queen was advised to invest in uranium.

Notwithstanding a green-wash, gamblers have no ethics –
And despite feigned concerns royalty knows that arms
Are good investments, and those with money always like making more –
Even if the whole planet becomes a death star

Through shells, and bombs and cruise missiles
All tipped with Depleted Uranium
So that they pierce more easily through the heavy armour
And the fortifications of fabricated enemies.

Air, water and soil are contaminated when DU is used.
Dr Doug Rokke, the ex-director of the Pentagon's
Depleted Uranium Project, says there is no way to
Decontaminate an area hit with uranium.

Yet Dr Jay Gould would reveal in his book, 'The Enemy Within',
The extent of royalty's uranium investments:
And their uranium wealth was hot-housed by an entrepreneur, Tiny Rowland,
Thanks to Rowland's companies Lonrho and Rio Tinto.

Tiny Rowland would asset-strip half of Africa –
And though this former Harrods bidder,
Was called "the unpleasant and unacceptable face of capitalism"
He was popular with royals and the mega-rich.

Never mind that Rowland was formerly Roland Walter Fuhrhop
An unashamed member of Hitler Youth –
Princess Alexandra's husband, the Queen's nephew, Angus Ogilvy,
Sat on Rowland's board with royal approval.

The royal shares would finance the arming of Africa
In Lonrho's resource wars:
African leaders who promised Lonrho strategic minerals
Were armed to the hilt by Ogilvy and Rowland.

Tiny Rowland was nicknamed "the royals' buccaneer"
And how much he made them is unknown
But the conditions of his African workforces were notorious,
As Africa fuelled a new spurt of royal wealth.

At Rowland's extractor plant in Ghana,
The Anti-Slavery Society reported in 1987,
Lonrho's Ashanti Goldmines employed
Sixty boys to work almost naked in pools of cyanide.

The cyanide used in separating out the gold
Enters the body as gas, liquid or acid dust;
The boys worked naked since, on Rowland's orders,
This was company policy, "to reduce theft".

In 1973 Lonrho was the biggest plantation owner in Africa
Controlling ninety-eight percent of oil imports through its pipelines.
It would mine, for example, forty percent of Zimbabwe's gold;
And it was the largest agricultural producer.

Thanks to their pet buccaneer, Royal shareholders
Were recolonizing Africa by the back door
And thanks to Tiny Rowland's helpful advice their uranium holdings
Are now worth more than six billion dollars.

But just as "England that was wont to conquer others", as Shakespeare wrote,
"Hath made a shameful conquest of herself"
Uranium winds can now blow back into the faces of profiteers
With its poisons being impossible to decontaminate.

Thanks to uranium investors, radioactive isotopes
Are now found in the flesh of worms:
At a Ministry of Defence weapons range in Dumfries
Depleted Uranium has turned the worms mutant.

Worms are a pillar of ecosystems through aerating the soil
And aiding the nutrient uptake of plants,
Whom Charles reputedly likes to talk to, though he may now need a Geiger counter
Before addressing the radioactive triffids of Scotland.

Unlike any hereditary monarchy however 'historic'
DU stains the environment for ever and ever;
Its half-life has earned it the title of a silent killer
"The silent killer that will never stop killing".

And there's nothing depleted about Depleted Uranium
When you see the birth defects it causes:
Swollen heads, enlarged eyeballs, dysfunctional limbs
As DU rewrites DNA codes, making them nonsense.

While the British government was waging its illegal war in Iraq
It increased the value of the royal investment
For the price of uranium would rise 500 percent in six years:
Its radioactive death-dance turns a profit.

When the East India Company defeated the Maharajah of Punjab,
The Company presented to Queen Victoria
The largest diamond ever to be discovered in the world
It was called the Koh-i-noor.

Later Queen Victoria would take a sadistic pleasure
In displaying the Koh-i-noor
To the Maharajah's heir on his visiting Buckingham Palace,
And he would leave muttering, "Mrs Fagin".

The criminal Fagin's profession in Dickens 'Oliver Twist'
Was as a receiver of stolen property
But unlike royalty, who receive stolen property with impunity,
Fagin's career would prove shorter lived.

Fagin was hanged at Newgate for his accumulated wealth,
Whereas the Queen continues to benefit
From assets which were once stolen from Simon de Montfort
And are now administered by the Duchy of Lancaster.

De Montfort was a rebel who wished to expand democracy
By undermining the power of the monarch
But such democratic concerns were rewarded by execution
And the confiscation of his property by the crown.

However de Montfort's corpse still produces dividends
From his 20,000 acres in Merseyside, which the crown seized;
And further lands in Yorkshire worth £72 million to the Queen
Are exempted from capital gains and corporation tax.

The crown also benefits handsomely from what's quaintly known
As the Duchy's "bona vacantia and bastardy funds".
A medieval mechanism whereby the Queen inherits the estates
Of all those in the Duchy who die intestate.

Thus this royal fund would do "surprisingly well"
As a result of the deaths of widows of soldiers
Who were killed in the Second World War, for their property
Would go to the very people who'd sent them to die.

In the year 2000 more than £2.1m was thus gleaned
For Her Majesty the Queen's private income
From 276 people from Merseyside and Lancashire –
They'd made no will, so their property was grabbed.

The estates of war veterans, the estates of the intestate
And also the proceeds of 232 companies,
Dissolved in the year 2000, their assets went to this lovable Queen:
A billionaire with an income from grave robbing.

And the same is true for the Duchy of Cornwall:
If you die without making a will
Everything you possess will go to Prince Charles —
To the billionaire biscuit-maker, plus his Duchess.

The threadbare convention that it's unfair to attack such a family
Is altogether redundant
For they answer back continuously and perfectly plainly,
With an untouchable mountain of money.

Money that impoverishes the rest of the country;
Money that serves to spread false values;
Money peddling creaky fantasies of storybook princes
Seeking out young virgins for chilly castles.

For monarchy means no more than the rule of money,
Overlaid by manipulative hokum:
A residual belief the Queen's queen by divine right,
All of which justifies inhuman riches.

But Royalty's not cricket when such accumulations of wealth
Are seen to cause others actual injury:
When, like slashing horses' flanks, they're allowed to haemorrhage
England's body politic with a thousand cuts.

It's clear that an acquisitive instinct is an endemic trait
In the British royal family's DNA:
When people heard, for example, that the Queen's grandmother, Mary,
Was threatening to come and stay with them,

They'd quickly hide their valuables and remove precious furniture
Just in case anything caught Queen Mary's eye
For she'd say that 'that would look well' in such-and-such room at Sandringham
Then order her ladies-in-waiting to have it 'sent on'.

Her hosts were left aghast; no compensation was offered
They could only resolve not to suffer her again –
Unlike the present-day public who repeatedly invite
Every royal kleptomaniac to rob them blind.

Queen Mary would always refer to her fellow royals
As 'dear so and so' with an approving nod,
Whereas she'd disdainfully preface the names of all commoners
With 'poor', as in 'poor Smith' or 'poor Jones'.

Her condescension was designed to reinforce
The bogus division she so clearly felt
Between people and 'unpeople' – exploiters 'like us'
And those others whom her class could exploit.

Yet royalty lacks even the courage of its own convictions
For as a social bond it's exposed as a sham:
When George V's first cousin, the Czar, begged for a safe haven for his family,
George V spurned him and they were all murdered.

But thanks to royalty's continuity, political thought is contaminated
By this surreal tumour within the state apparatus –
Whereby no one's interests can ever fairly be represented
When a country's distorted by a royalty mania.

The former Labour MP Glenda Jackson once protested
"My constituents are angry about where their country is going,
But you would never know their concerns from press coverage,
Which is," she despaired, "obsessed with royalty."

It's even forbidden to demonstrate outside a royal palace
Or at any one of the three hundred royal properties;
Those who do so are locked up, along with the sad stalkers
Who haunt such places, thinking royals are supernatural.

A 'Not the Royal Wedding' street party in Covent Garden
Was banned by London's 'leftist' Camden Council:
Who claimed since local businesses objected they'd have to wield a stick
To protect this precious superstition from satire.

Likewise, Clarence House insisted that Australia's ABC network
Dropped its plans to broadcast a comic wedding commentary:
A royal decree forbade use of any live footage
In a 'comedy, satirical or similar programme'.

Yet while innocuous jesters such as 'Mr Bean' were invited
To dance attendance upon this 'special event'
An anti-joker police force ring-fenced Westminster Abbey
With a mile deep sterile zone, a humour by-pass.

Tom Paine said hereditary power was as implausible
As having hereditary mathematicians,
And Ben Franklin compared monarchy to the potato since any goodness,
Like old kings and queens, lay underground –

The initial role of a 'king', deriving from the word 'kindred',
Was once to be the tribe's highest common factor –
But when virtue's traded for war profiteering and the rest
Then its bubble can be said to have burst.

In *The Ancient Mariner* Coleridge wrote of a man doomed
By his having killed an albatross;
A similar curse attaches to the Ibis, the slow, celestial bird
Revered in hieroglyphs for changing the tides.

In Egypt the moon god Thoth would appear as an Ibis
And with his wife, Maat, Thoth made a cosmic egg.
It was to feed the sun god with an harmonious essence
And its bounty would pervade and support creation.

Aeons later, a fake 'House of Windsor', a less magical fable,
Built on flyblown genealogies has to crumble,
With its offspring being turned out of their gilded cages
And allowing the wildlife they persecute to fly free.

It's said that you should be careful for what you wish for
In case it should ever come true
Yet surely no one need be restrained from removing a cancer
Until they've found a replacement.

For once cauterized the royal disease can be switched
For something that can be much healthier
Just by totting up the family's monumental mountains of wealth
And turning them into a people's portfolio.

For after thirty generations of armed, bejewelled parasites,
Beginning with the Norman conquest,
And after monarchs using their office for non-stop acquisition
The royal riches are now nearly incalculable.

But someone could easily be found to turn Queen's evidence,
Then to undertake a fiscal fishing expedition
In which no stone's unturned until every possession
Has been converted into a people's inheritance.

Making a start with royal property in Manhattan,
Left over from colonial days;
There are acres in South Carolina with stud farms attached
And then there are lands and properties

All over Britain and throughout London, in Belgravia
And Chelsea and Mayfair and Hampstead and Fulham
And Greenwich and Clapham, and everywhere...
Where property prices are astronomical.

The richest family in Europe in the 14th century
Bore the surname of Guelph
And it's from the Guelphs that this family's descended
And their wealth has expanded ever since.

On a state visit to Canada, the Duke of Edinburgh
Said Canada was "a good investment"
Wherever the royals travel they are always alive
To an opportunity for remuneration.

They own property in Canada, Australia and Africa;
In the Far East and New Zealand, and much more
Thanks to the device of 'Bank of England Nominees'
Whereby heads of state can buy shares secretly.

But for one family to own unlimited global assets
And huge chunks of a clutch of small islands
Upon which there are large tracts of deprivation
Flies in the face of all natural justice.

Yet there are Rembrandts, tiaras and diamonds in strong-rooms
(Some ghoulishly derived from the Czar)
Then there are sheaves of stocks and dubious holdings
Often hidden behind surrogate names.

The crown's a subtle halo to sanctify these assets:
The crown marks out its property with a taboo
As if to say 'you can't touch any of our possessions –
They're protected by the state's darkest spells'.

So to find out where all the treasure's hidden.
Be it in Swiss banks or in the Bahamas
Would be challenging, but as banks spill the beans
The beans can be gathered up and cashed in.

The money's reclamation would only require the same mechanisms
Used to track down the proceeds of crime
Royal wealth is just the same: it's a corrosive talisman
Swindling citizens into becoming subjects.

Once done, the billions in assets and in real estate
Would provide each man, woman and child
With a basic income as their guaranteed birthright.
It would become their due as citizen stakeholders.

Instead of twenty million in the UK being below the poverty line,
Instead of their life-expectancy being shortened,
Instead of their inequality being just their bad luck
The royal nest egg could be a national omelette.

Tom Paine first floated the idea of 'Basic Income'
At the end of the eighteenth century.
He proposed it while composing 'The Rights of Man'
Then it was taken up by Thomas Spence.

For you don't have a society if it's run by spivs and shysters
With royalty accentuating such divisions:
'Do people actually live here?' said Princess Margaret's lady-in-waiting
As the royal party passed through Peterhead.

"Don't you know who I am?" Prince Charles once snapped
When his former wife objected to his behaviour.
She clearly thought his question wasn't worth answering
So she left without ever returning.

And when a comprehensive inventory's been done,
With all royal secrecy being dissolved,
Then re-empowered citizens can have ready access
And given an idea of what they've been missing.

A present guesstimate has royal assets being worth
Hundreds and hundreds of billions:
Six thousand billion has been mentioned as a ball-park sum;
Yielding everyone ten thousand a year for life.

To dissolve the Crown Estates alone would produce billions:
For every offshore wind-farm's electricity
Could then enrich people power and not hereditary privilege –
Since coastal rents needn't be paid to the monarch.

Just as the family's capable of renouncing its German identity
And declaring its name to be 'Windsor'
(So as to capitalize on Windsor's connection to Arthur's round table),
It can just as easily forego its fraudulent wealth.

It could even be thought of as its religious duty
Since the ostensible Head of the Church
Must know of its founder's views on social justice:
Jesus would want his royal fans to divvy up.

In any case, idle notions of royal bloodlines are unchristian:
The book of Acts 17: 26 states clearly,
"And hath made of one blood all nations of men
For to dwell on all the face of the earth",

In other words no so-called royal bloodline is special
For everyone can be as royal as they choose:
Duke Ellington, Earl Hines, Old King Cole and King Crimson
Show everyone's already an aristocrat.

Common sense tells any but the most delusional
That there are no kings, just talking tiaras –
Whose diamonds are likely to be encrusted with blood
Making all of them morally toxic.

But bowing down to bejewelled wealth creates a poverty
Since it impoverishes humanity itself
For when sparkling rocks are clawed out of the earth by virtual slaves
The message of such royal 'bling' is that you can own people.

The royal wealth has slowly disembowelled England
Economically ravaging its true heritage
Yet if Robin Hood and Shelley and Blake and Tom Paine were its mentors
Britain could decontaminate its radioactive crown, and be rid of it.

"The man of virtuous soul," Shelley wrote
"Commands not, nor obeys.
Power, like a desolating pestilence,
Pollutes whatever it touches;

"And obedience, bane of all genius,
Virtue, freedom, truth,
Makes slaves of men, and of the human frame.
A mechanized automaton."

The world's sheepish subjects wave repetitively
At the privileged in their golden boxes,
'Look, the Queen!' they'll say, again and again,
Without seeing the elephant in the room.

Those bathing in the stardust of the state fetishes
Ensure the creaky show trundles on
Then a royal wedding rebrands the charade
As does a visit to Hollywood's tinseltown.

The celluloid marionettes of LaLa Land
That lubricate another Empire.
Fawn over their fellow celebrities and forget about
US independence from the crown.

Yet now these two heirs to ritual wealth and status
Inherit a sixth of the world's land mass,
They own Canada, they own Australia and the rest
In exchange the world gets some forced smiles.

The queen is the largest landowner in history
With 6,600 million acres worldwide,
Her killer heirs will wish to increase the royal holdings
Though it's time every acre was returned.

The former editor of the left wing *Daily Mirror,*
Now an American chat show host, tells *Sky News*
That "William and Kate are the biggest stars in the world,"
He fawningly chronicles their playing polo in Hollywood

And their shaking hands with movie star after movie star
Then giving a royal blessing to veterans of US wars
Before the royalty-mongering Morgan declares that,
'The impact they've had on Hollywood shows they're stars"

But his grovelling merely sells out England to Hollywood,
The PR wing of the US Empire,
Whose Dracula hedge-funds suck the world dry
And whose wars keep a death-culture in business.

The show goes on. William tells US veterans
He "knows what war is about"
And has said that he's passionately keen to go to war.
Adding he's not keen on being overshadowed

By his bloodthirsty brother Harry in Afghanistan
And that he too, William – Diana's "thug" –
Wishes to participate in the same spurious killing sprees
(In what are squalid race wars over resources).

His wife's fashionable 'Shola' dress is shown off in walkabouts
When it's reported that 'everyone wants one'
Though it's made in a Romanian sweatshop whose workers
Are paid ninety-nine pence an hour.

But in Montreal some Native Canadians see through it all:
Exclaiming "la monarchie – personne a voté pour ça"
(Monarchy – nobody voted for that). They hold a banner
With four welcoming words, 'ROYAL PARASITES! GO HOME!'

As if cursed, royalty become the animals they've killed –
Zoo animals to be stared at by tourists –
Catnip for those 'anxious for a glimpse of history'
Though history's made outside of such museums.

The Queen and the Queen's mother are filmed by George VI
Making that Nazi gesture that's so uniquely vile
And the picture goes viral as if the penny's finally dropped
About this unholy family's redundant mind-set.

When the Queen was once asked if the monster –
The creature that lives in Loch Ness –
Could be called 'Elizabeth Nessia' this was rejected
As she "couldn't lend her name to a possible hoax".

And yet the monarchy has been just that for generations:
Ordinary people taking part in a confidence trick
That seeks to elevate them above other human beings
Aided by superstition, military force and by habit.

A Republican Garner

If a psychiatric and scientific inquiry were to be made upon our rulers, mankind would be appalled at the disclosures.
ALFRED KORZYBSKI

'Who made thee a prince and a judge over us?'
EXODUS. II. 14.

"Simhasan Khali Karo, Janta aati hai" (Vacate the throne, the people are coming)
RAMDHARI SINGH 'DINKAR', HINDI POET

"Break in pieces quickly the Band of particular Propriety [property], disown this oppressing Murder, Oppression and Thievery of Buying and Selling of Land, owning of landlords and paying of Rents and give thy Free Consent to make the Earth a Common Treasury without grumbling...that all may enjoy the benefit of their Creation. Propriety and single interest divides the people of a land and the whole world into parties and is the cause of all wars and bloodshed and contention everywhere."
GERRARD WINSTANLEY & 14 OTHERS 'THE TRUE LEVELLERS STANDARD ADVANCED', APRIL, 1649

"For all men being originally equals, no one by birth could have a right to set up his own family in perpetual preference to all others for ever, and though himself might deserve some decent degree of honors of his contemporaries, yet his descendants might be far too unworthy to inherit them.

One of the strongest natural proofs of the folly of hereditary right in kings, is, that nature disapproves it, otherwise she would not so frequently turn it into ridicule by giving mankind an ass for a lion."
THOMAS PAINE, *COMMON SENSE*, 1776

"The people who are in control and in power and the class system and the whole bullshit bourgeois scene is exactly the same... The same bastards are in control, the same people are running everything, it's exactly the same... people are living in fucking poverty with rats crawling over them, it's the same. It just makes you puke."
JOHN LENNON, INTERVIEWED IN *ROLLING STONE*, 1970

"I would argue that television and particularly the BBC were instrumental in puffing up the Royal Family to a level where they were inflated out of all proportion to their relevance on the national scene."
ANDREW MORTON

"Put not your trust in princes."
PSALMS, CXLVI. 3.

"The monarchy is finished. It was finished a while ago, but they're still making the corpses dance."
SUE TOWNSEND

"The anachronistic absurdity of Britain's royal family, with its vast inherited wealth and theoretical power cannot be touched. No public figure who governs or hopes to govern can go near the issue, whatever their personal views.

Instead they must pay homage, bow or curtsy when the time comes, and never question why it is that inherited peerages are abolished but the Queen opens Parliament every year and appoints a prime minister after an election on the basis of the hereditary principle, or why inherited wealth is viewed with a degree of wariness, at least in relation to most other people but not to those born into this particular family."

'Our republican conspiracy of silence: No public figure that governs, or hopes to govern can go near the issue. It would be the end of their careers'.
STEVE RICHARDS, LONDON: THE INDEPENDENT, APRIL, 21, 2011

"If you think that moth-eaten monarchy of yours is gonna keep the lid on this powder-keg, you got another think comin'"
WILLIAM S. BURROUGHS, IN CONVERSATION, LONDON, 1968

"Of the various forms of government which have prevailed in the world, an hereditary monarchy seems to present the fairest scope for ridicule."
EDWARD GIBBON

"*Dennis the Peasant:* 'Listen. Strange women lying in ponds distributing swords is no basis for a system of government. Supreme executive power derives from a mandate from the masses, not from some farcical aquatic ceremony.'

King Arthur: 'Be quiet!'

Dennis: 'You can't expect to wield supreme power just 'cause some watery tart threw a sword at you!'"
MONTY PYTHON AND THE HOLY GRAIL

"I didn't want to attack the monarchy in a sort of beer monster way," he [Morrissey] explains [...] "But I find as time goes by, this happiness we had slowly slips away and is replaced by something that is wholly grey and wholly saddening.

The very idea of the monarchy and the Queen of England is being reinforced and made to seem more useful than it really is."

I suggest that the hardest thing to stomach about the monarchy these days is the way they're increasingly used as political camouflage. Five million unemployed? Have another Royal Wedding, chaps.

Oh yes it's disgusting. When you consider what minimal contribution they make in helping people. They never under any circumstances make a useful statement about the world or people's lives. The whole thing seems like a joke, a hideous joke. We don't believe in leprechauns so why should we believe in the Queen?"

MORRISSEY INTERVIEWED BY IAN PYE, *NEW MUSICAL EXPRESS*, JUNE 7, 1986.

"The Royal family to me are not England, and they are not the flag. The Queen is the ultimate dictator. And it is dictatorship. It's forced upon the British people. And if the British people decided tomorrow that the Queen must go, the Queen wouldn't hesitate to turn her tanks on the British people. It would happen. Because the police are commissioned to protect the Queen against the people of England. That's their first and foremost task. And I find that absolutely absurd."

MORRISSEY

"Why would I watch the wedding? I couldn't take any of that seriously. I don't think the so-called Royal family speak for England now, and I don't think England needs them.

I do seriously believe that they are benefit scroungers, nothing else. I don't believe they serve any purpose whatsoever. I'm not an anarchist, but I believe that people don't want the Royal family -- the so-called Royal family. They're not royal to me, but they're royal to the media for some reason."

MORRISSEY, INTERVIEWED BY JOHN WILSON ON FRONT ROW, BBC RADIO FOUR

In his 1986 epic "The Queen Is Dead," which launched the album of the same name, Morrissey shot broadsides against the family.

"The very idea of Charles being King is laughable. You might as well say that Ronnie Corbett will be king one day. I think that would give people more pleasure."
HTTP://WWW.HUFFINGTONPOST.COM/2011/04/28/MORRISSEY-BLASTS-ROYAL-WEDDING-FAMILY_N_854837.HTML

"The Tories in England had long imagined that they were enthusiastic about the monarchy, the church and beauties of the old English Constitution, until the day of danger wrung from them the confession that they are enthusiastic only about rent."
KARL MARX

"It was pitiful for a person born in a wholesome free atmosphere to listen to their humble and hearty outpourings of loyalty toward their king and Church and nobility; as if they had any more occasion to love and honor king and Church and noble than a slave has to love and honor the lash, or a dog has to love and honor the stranger that kicks him!

Why, dear me, ANY kind of royalty, howsoever modified, ANY kind of aristocracy, howsoever pruned, is rightly an insult; but if you are born and brought up under that sort of arrangement you probably never find it out for yourself, and don't believe it when somebody else tells you. It is enough to make a body ashamed of his race to think of the sort of froth that has always occupied its thrones without shadow of right or reason, and the seventh-rate people that have always figured as its aristocracies -- a company of monarchs and nobles who, as a rule, would have achieved only poverty and obscurity if left, like their betters, to their own exertions...

The truth was, the nation as a body was in the world for one object, and one only: to grovel before king and Church and noble; to slave

for them, sweat blood for them, starve that they might be fed, work
that they might play, drink misery to the dregs that they might be
happy, go naked that they might wear silks and jewels, pay taxes that
they might be spared from paying them, be familiar all their lives
with the degrading language and postures of adulation that they
might walk in pride and think themselves the gods of this world.
And for all this, the thanks they got were cuffs and contempt; and
so poor-spirited were they that they took even this sort of attention
as an honor."
MARK TWAIN

"What! You say a horse is noble because it is good in itself, and the
same you say of a falcon of a pearl; but a man shall be called noble
because his ancestors were so? Not with words, but with knives must
one answer such a beastly notion."
DANTE ALIGHIERI

"I have been told all my life by the existence of a monarchy that I am
an inferior creature and that regardless of my intellect, efforts and
hard work I will never be equal to someone who was born better than
me and always will be. That is the message that having a monarchy
sends and you can see it everyday in the baying sycophancy of royalist
media. It's time to start debating (an end to the monarchy) now."
GRAHAM SMITH, REPUBLIC

"I believe in aristocracy — if that is the right word, and if a democrat
may use it — though not an aristocracy of power, based upon rank
and influence, but an aristocracy of the sensitive, the considerate and
the plucky. Its members are to be found in all nations and classes, and
all through the ages, and there is a secret understanding between them
when they meet. They represent the true human tradition, the one
permanent victory of our queer race over cruelty and chaos.

Thousands of them perish in obscurity, a few are great names.
They are sensitive for others as well as themselves, they are
considerate without being fussy, their pluck is not swankiness
but power to endure, and they can take a joke."
E.M. Forster, *Two Cheers For Democracy*

"….a moral and intellectual weakling [Prince Charles] from the
usurping House of Hanover. An awful embarrassment awaits the
British if they do not declare for a republic."
Christopher Hitchens, 'Charles, Prince of Piffle', Slate, 8
August, 2010

But if men would live up to reason's rules,

They would not bow and scrape to wealthy fools.
Lucretius, 95-52 B.C.

Twll din I'r Tywysog Cymru
(Welsh T-shirt. 'Arseholes to the Prince of Wales')

"You don't write a song like 'God Save The Queen' because you hate
the English race. You write a song like that because you love them,
and you're fed up of seeing them mistreated."

Johnny Rotten/John Lydon, Sex Pistols Vinyl Reissues 2007:
'God Save The Queen'

"It is a strange fact, but it is unquestionably true, that almost any
English intellectual would feel more ashamed of standing to attention
during "God Save the King" than stealing from a poor box".
George Orwell

"You that love England, who have an ear for her music,

Listen. Can you not hear the entrance of a new theme?"
C Day Lewis, *You That Love England* (1933)

Ach 'se seallech leointe is gann

Tha an seo aig ceann thall an linn

Talann alainn nan daoine

Fhathast am lamhan duine no dithis

(But it's a wounding and a hollow sight

Here as we reach the end of the century

The beautiful soul of the people

Still in the hands of the few.)

'ALBA' RUNRIG,

'All things begin and end in Albion's ancient, Druid rocky shore.'
WILLIAM BLAKE

"There is more stupidity than hydrogen in the world, and it has a
longer shelf life."
FRANK ZAPPA

Queen Elizabeth II, the largest landowner on Earth.

"Queen Elizabeth II, head of state of the United Kingdom and of 31 other states and territories, is the legal owner of about 6,600 million acres of land, one sixth of the earth's non ocean surface. She is the only person on earth who owns whole countries, and who owns countries that are not her own domestic territory. This land ownership is separate from her role as head of state and is different from other monarchies where no such claim is made − Norway, Belgium, Denmark etc. The value of her land holding. £17,600,000,000,000 (approx). This makes her the richest individual on earth. However, there is no way easily to value her real estate. There is no current market in the land of entire countries. At a rough estimate of $5,000 an acre, and based on the sale of Alaska to the USA by the Tsar, and of Louisiana to the USA by France, the Queen's land holding is worth a notional $33,000,000,000,000 (Thirty three trillion dollars or about £17,600,000,000,000). Her holding is based on the laws of the countries she owns and her land title is valid in all the countries she owns. Her main holdings are Canada, the 2nd largest country on earth, with 2,467 million acres, Australia, the 7th largest country on earth with 1,900 million acres, the Papua New Guinea with114 million acres, New Zealand with 66 million acres and the UK with 60 million acres. She is the world's largest landowner by a significant margin. The next largest landowner is the Russian state, with an overall ownership of 4,219 million acres, and a direct ownership comparable with the Queen's land holding of 2,447 million acres. The 3rd largest landowner is the Chinese state, which claims all of Chinese land, about 2,365 million acres. The 4th largest landowner on earth is the Federal Government of the United States, which owns about one third of the land of the USA, 760 million acres. The fifth largest landowner on earth is the King of Saudi Arabia with 553 million acres.

LARGEST FIVE PERSONAL LANDOWNERS ON EARTH.

- Queen Elizabeth II 6,600 million acres

- King Abdullah of Saudi Arabia 553 million acres

- King Bhumibol of Thailand 126 million acres

- King Mohammed IV of Morocco 113 million acres

- Sultan Quaboos of Oman 76 million acres."

http://www.whoownstheworld.com/about-the-book/largest-landowner/

Sources

"interrupt the grouse season at Balmoral"

"When Britain declared war on Germany he [George VI] expressed concern that the crisis might interfere with the Balmoral grouse season." Karl Shaw, *Royal Babylon: The Alarming History of European Royalty.* New York: Broadway Books, 1999, p. 280

"enabler of Britain's centuries-long killing sprees."

John Kampfner, 'Profile – David Manning', London: *New Statesman*, 23 September 2002

"her share portfolio, with a personal fortune totaling £290m"

Sunday Times Rich List: Super-rich grew wealthier in recession, "The fortunes of the wealthiest 1,000 people in Britain rose by 30 per cent despite the recession, the Sunday Times Rich List has shown. (25 Apr 2010)." Telegraph.co.uk, Friday 29 April 2011

"horses drugged with acepromazine
So that they may be kept compliant throughout"

The People, 14 February 1999

"minor royals exercising the *droit de seigneur.*
Entering their quarters to treat them as sexual chattels."

And They Wonder Why We Hate Them, Facebook/ http://reocities.com/CapitolHill/lobby/1793/news.html – "10.01.99 - THE NEWS OF THE WORLD describes how Prince Edward maintained the tradition of using Royal servants as sexual chattels."

"for a further £500,000 she'll provide
An introduction to her husband Prince Andrew"

Heather Brooke, 'Royal appetite for secrecy can only invite scandal', *Guardian*, 25 May 2010,

"For their impudence in exposing bribery in Saudi arms deals"

http://watchingyouwatchingyme-steelmagnolia.
blogspot.com/2010/12/royal-parasite-prince-andrew.html

http://www.theguardian.com/commentisfree /
libertycentral/2010/may/24/royal-appetite-secrecy-only-invite-scandal

"'enhanced compliance processes' Which in any case, said the Prince, should be legalized."

http://www.dailymail.co.uk/news/
article-1334223/WIKILEAKS-Vince-Cable-tells-Prince-Andrew-steer-clear-politics.
html#ixzz1S4gSin00

"'Rude' Prince Andrew flies to New York to face Americans he insulted as Vince Cable tells him to steer clear of politics"

"Prince Andrew used his royal position to demand a special briefing from the Serious Fraud Office weeks before launching a tirade against the agency's "idiotic" investigators at a lunch with businessmen in Kyrgyzstan." *Guardian*, 30 November 2011

"Because his monogrammed towels aren't replaced Immediately after the prince has used them."

Ingrid Seward, 'A very pampered Prince', *Evening Standard*, London: 14 November 2002,

"That "pigs' ears are still not making silk purses".

Sunday Mercury, Birmingham: December 31, 2001, George Tyndale:
'Princess of Bad Manners,'

"Our inorganic world's disharmony"

A correspondence along these lines between Charles and the antiquarian occultist John Michell, was found amongst John Michell's papers by Jonangus Mackay who was editing a festschrift devoted to Michell's work, 'Michelliana'.

"As there are not very many big ones left."

Karl Shaw, *Royal Babylon: The Alarming History of European Royalty*. New York: Broadway Books, 1999, p. 280

"...Then the stag's head was severed For it to have pride of place at Balmoral."

"For more than a century the walls of the Queen's Highland stronghold, Balmoral Castle, have been covered with stags' head trophies bagged by royal ancestors. The Queen herself fell in love with stalking when she shot her first stag with her father King George VI in 1945, at the age of 16. Her governess Marion Crawford recalled the Princess's excitement of that day."

Karl Shaw, *Royal Babylon: The Alarming History of European Royalty*. New York: Broadway Books, 1999

"...and an Indian tiger."

The Independent, London, 20 December 1996, Paul Vallely, 'Out of touch - by definition'

"...killed 50 wild boar in a single day."

The Independent, London: 20 December 1996, Jojo Moyes, 'Royals' shooting passion draws bad blood: Prince reconciles longstanding enthusiasm with role for nature charity'

"so keen on killing things"

http://goliath.ecnext.com/coms2/gi_0199-8509156/WILLIAM-S-FIRST-KILL-1.html

"I'm going to send my knights around to kill you."

Ingrid Seward, *William and Harry: a portrait of two princes*, Headline, 2003. p.88

"I'll get my dad to cut your head off."

Ingrid Seward, *William and Harry: a portrait of two princes*, Headline, 2003. p. 171

"...Who does not want you to shoot Bambis."

Ingrid Seward, *William and Harry: a portrait of two princes*, Headline, 2003.p.103-4

"...than when they have a gun in their hands."

Ingrid Seward, *William and Harry: a portrait of two princes*, Headline, 2003.p.221

"I was told they were good enough to eat."

Terence Blacker, 'Woe to he who kills the sacred ibis,' London: *The Independent*, 17 July 2001

"urged him to watch a kill"

News of the World, 31 October 1999

"And all envelopes were handled with gloves"

Much of the historical detail in this list derives from '*Twelve Mad Monarchs, First 10*' which appeared, uncredited, in *Time Out* November 1998, then was later amended and re-titled, '*And they wonder why we hate them*' and republished on the website 'Ma'am, the Movement against the Monarchy'

"Her opposition to the lucrative peddling of landmines"

i) Laura Harding, PA, 'Diana death 'linked to arms trade' says QC,' *The Independent*, 31 May 2010

ii) *Mail Foreign Service*. "Princess Diana 'was killed after plan to frighten her went wrong'", *Daily Mail*, 12th March 2010 "Princess Diana died after attempts to frighten her into dumping Dodi al Fayed and ending her anti-establishment activities went horribly wrong, a leading lawyer has claimed. Michael Mansfield claimed he was sure Diana's 'killers' had no intention of ending her life in a Paris tunnel in August 1997 and simply wanted to scare her.

But he claimed the operation to torpedo her relationship with Dodi, and silence her planned criticism of the British government over foreign arms sales, backfired spectacularly."

"That sends me to her *Kingdom* Come. Can you dig it?"

As relayed to the author by John Michell, recounting a conversation with Michael that took place on Death Row, Royal Gaol, Trinidad, in May 1975; cf also William Levy and John Michell (edd.) *Souvenir Programme for the Official Lynching of Michael Abdul Malik with poems, stories, sayings by the condemned*, Cambridge: 1973

"But Queen say, 'One to hang.'"

There was a fevered atmosphere in Trinidad at the time. Some local commentators portrayed

Michael –in his role as fugitive firebrand and quondam UK Black Power leader with high profile friends , such as John Lennon and Dick Gregory – as a political threat to Trinidad's mild mannered and scholarly Prime Minister, Eric Williams. The gruesome events in Michael's Arima commune and his trial reports prompted various songs, such as this one, all very much like those which appeared in the *Newgate Calendar* (subtitled *The Malefactors' Bloody Register*) in the 18th and 19th Centuries, and in the chapbooks devoted to the careers of Jonathan Wild, Dick Turpin and Moll Cutpurse sold to the Tyburn crowds who'd gathered to watch their executions at what was then a public spectacle.

'One to hang' a soca calypso, was written by Aldwyn Roberts (18 April 1922 - 11 February 2000), better known as Lord Kitchener or 'Kitch', and recorded on Ice Records, Barbados (no date).

"Had been signed by the Queen on the 14th May,'75"

John L. Williams, *Michael X: A Life in Black & White*, London: Century (p 270) "...they [the Law Lords] delivered their judgment, and had it signed by the Queen, two days later her instructions were conveyed to the Governor General in a record-breaking two weeks, on 14th May, a Wednesday."

"This is no place for you, pretty girl."

Geoffrey Robertson, *The Justice Game*, 1998, cited in John L. Williams op cit. p 271

"To see the conditions his people were living in."

Derek Humphrey & David Tindall, *False Messiah*, London: Hart-Davis. MacGibbbon, 1977, cited in John L. Williams, op. cit, p.205

"To the poems of Allen Ginsberg or Muhammad Ali."

From the papers of the American Committee to Save Michael X, founded by Dan Richter, cf John L Williams, op cit p 261

"But instead of an 'X' they added graveyard crosses."

It is not the issue here, but regarding Michael X's guilt a recent biography, John L Williams, *Michael X: A Life in Black & White*, London: Century, 2008, pp 236-7 reveals that Greville Plugge,

the twin brother of Gale Benson with whose murder Michael was charged, "told friends that he suspected that Michael was not the killer." According to a house guest, Trina Simmonds, who was staying at the Trinidad commune, which Michael had established on his leaving England with financial help from John Lennon and Yoko Ono, Gale Benson's relationship with her boyfriend, Hakim Jamal had broken down because of Gale's infidelity, and "Hakim and Gale had been arguing the night before her death." However the main suspect, Hakim Jamal, was never interviewed by the Trinidad police. "Hakim was asked to return to Trinidad [from Boston] to give a witness statement but unsurprisingly, he never did so. So the most obvious suspect for Gale's murder was never brought to trial." "The Trinidad police [...]} seemed strangely uninterested in charging Hakim with Gale's murder, even as an accessory [...] All Trinidad simply assumed that he [Michael] was guilty. As a result Michael found it hard to find adequate representation."

"To glamorize their country's war and to attract recruits."

Prince Harry 'directs his first bomb attack', London: *Daily Telegraph*, 28 Feb 2008

"He's then thought to have boasted of it afterwards."

http://bp2.blogger.com/_J3TsuLwgS94/ R8mkOgnlfuI/AAAAAAAAIY/ eH1NPiaErNg/s1600-h/Harry+Kills+30.jpg

David Williams, 'The moment Harry directed his first bomb attack on Terry Taliban for 'Kill TV'' London: *Daily Mail*, 29 February 2008

"For it concerned her to be a fraction less wealthy."

Heather Stewart, economics editor, 'This is how we let the credit crunch happen, Ma'am', London: *The Observer*, 26 July 2009

"It would be a tragic thing for the world If [Adolf] Hitler were overthrown".

December 1940 – In an interview with an American journalist, for the US magazine *Liberty*, Edward states, "It would be a tragic thing for the world if Hitler were overthrown."cited in Kitty Kelly, op cit. p. 22

SOURCES PAGES 18-23

http://channel.nationalgeographic.com/
episode/britain-s-nazi-king-4586/
timeline#ixzz11xm4MXKF

Leaving their country of origin."

Avraham Reiss, 'King George VI Tightened
the Noose Around German Jewry's Neck'
Jewish Chronicle, October 18, 2010

"To check the unauthorized emigration of Jews."

"In the spring of 1939 George VI instructed his
private secretary to write to Foreign Secretary
Lord Halifax. Having learnt that 'a number
of Jewish refugees from different countries
were surreptitiously getting into Palestine', the
King was 'glad to think that steps are being
taken to prevent these people leaving their
country of origin.' Halifax's office telegraphed
Britain's ambassador in Berlin asking him to
encourage the German government 'to check
the unauthorized emigration' of Jews." Ben
Summerskill, "MPs Want Quick Release of
Queen Mother's Papers," *The Observer,* Sunday
14 April 2002

"inhibited about the Jews"

As told by Philip to Deutsche Press Agentur
in August 1988; he reiterated his desire to
be a catalyst for mass genocide in the
foreword to his book *If I Were an Animal,*
Robin Clark Ltd., 1986.

In July 1983, Philip chastised aid workers and
charities for helping to treat malaria victims in
Sri Lanka.

"…Philip's featuring at Nazi funerals."

"Funeral procession in Darmstadt on 19
November 1937 after the airplane crash that
killed seven members of the Hesse-Darmstadt
family. Leading the procession is the heir, Prince
Ludwig von Hessen Darmstadt. The second row
consists of, from left to right, Prince 'Friedel'
Hohenlohe, Prince Christoph von Hessen (in
an SS uniform), Prince Philip current duke of
Edinburgh), and Prince Berthold von Baden.
Lord Louis Mountbatten follows in a peaked
naval cap in the row behind. Note that members
of the crowd make the Nazi salute."

Jonathan Petropoulos, *The Royals and the Reich:
The Princes von Hessen in Nazi Germany,* OUP,
2006, p. 95

"Would doubtless have been common currency."

Jonathan Petropoulos, *The Royals and the Reich:
The Princes von Hessen in Nazi Germany,* OUP,
2006, p. 133

**"In the hope of assassinating George and
reinstating Edward."**

Jonathan Petropoulos, *Royals and the Reich: The Princes
von Hessen in Nazi Germany,* OUP, 2003, p.11

**"Blunt's own brand of treason was granted
immunity."**

"In the final days of World War II in Europe,
Blunt made a successful secret trip to Schloss
Friedrichshof in Germany to retrieve sensitive
letters between the Duke of Windsor and
Adolf Hitler and other leading Nazis."
Blunt's Wikipedia entry, cf Charles Higham
(1988), *The Duchess of Windsor: The Secret Life,*
New York: McGraw-Hill Publishers 1988,
pp. 388–389; and Peter Wright, *Spycatcher:
The Autobiography of a Senior Intelligence Officer,*
Toronto: Stoddart Publishers , 1987

"I would like to return as a deadly virus"

'Did I say that?' Prince Philip, the Queen's
consort , quotes compiled by John Hind,
London: *The Observer,* 21 June 2009

**"…Of U.S. foreign policy towards the
Third World."**

National Security Council (NSC) Memo 200,
dated April 24, 1974, and titled "Implications
of world wide population growth for U.S.
security and overseas interests," states:

"Dr Henry Kissinger proposed in his
memorandum to the NSC that 'depopulation
should be the highest priority of U.S. foreign
policy towards the Third World.'

He quoted reasons of national security, and
because "(t)he U.S. economy will require
large and increasing amounts of minerals
from abroad, especially from less-developed
countries ... Wherever a lessening of
population can increase the prospects for such
stability, population policy becomes relevant
to resources, supplies and to the economic
interests of U.S."

"You need to go back to the colonies."

Baron Gunther von Reibnitz, the father of

Princess Michael of Kent, was a party member and an honorary member of the SS.

"I don't want to meet any daft children."

Kitty Kelly, *The Royals*, New York: Warner Books, pp. 1-4

"As either "blackamoors" or else 'nig nogs.'"

Kitty Kelly op. cit. p. 24

"…Swept his Duchy of Cornwall estate."

Andrew Buckwell, 'The Final Straw; Charles' rent demand could push farmers over edge', London: *Sunday Mirror*, Mar 11, 2001

"This could push our members over the edge."

Andrew Buckwell, Royal Correspondent, 'The Final Straw, Charles' rent demand could push farmers over edge, "PRINCE Charles was last night accused of driving his tenant farmers towards suicide with a £2.3million rent demand as foot- and-mouth swept his Duchy of Cornwall estate. The warning came as the Prince's office insisted it was "business as usual" on his estate, despite the deepening national crisis." London: *Sunday Mirror*, Mar 11, 2001

"The Duchy is sympathetic as long as you pay the rent."

"If you lose all your stock and are feeling pretty down, a rent demand is the last thing you want to see." Andy [Bradford] who has worked his farm since 1969, said: "The Duchy is sympathetic as long as you pay the rent." Andrew Buckwell, 'The Final Straw; Charles' rent demand could push farmers over edge,' *Sunday Mirror*, Mar 11, 2001

Applauds those carrying nuclear payloads as "heroes"

Richard Palmer, Royal Correspondent, 'Prince William, the dashing officer, honours our Trident heroes: Prince William saluted the sailors responsible for maintaining Trident at a naval base.' London: Daily Express, October 29, 2010

"Believed the Queen had invented the telephone."

"One in 10 children thinks the Queen invented the telephone, a survey of children's science knowledge suggests". BBC, 13 March 2010 http://news.bbc.co.uk/1/hi/education/8565258.stm

"The US general, who said Iraq's dead 'weren't worth counting'"

During the 1991 Gulf War, General H Norman Schwarzkopf, top commander of US and allied forces and a combat veteran of two tours of the Vietnam War, repeatedly denied tallying enemy dead. "Body count means nothing," Schwartzkopf told reporters. "Absolutely nothing."

David Axe 'US counts enemy dead and it's not reassuring', Irish Examiner, January, 23, 2015

"For what the Cambodians did to each other?"

Henry Kissinger, with Richard Nixon, was responsible for the massive bombing of Cambodia in 1973, which killed three-quarters of a million peasants and disrupted Cambodian society, setting the stage for Pol Pot to come to power and ultimately kill another one-and-a-half million people. His remark was made on 7 March 1999 in an interview with Leslie Stahl on the CBS news program *60 Minutes.*

"I want every Iraqi soldier bleeding from every orifice."

Schwartzkopf's sanguinary ambition in the Gulf War, as expressed to his division commanders and cited in Rick Atkinson, *Crusade: The Untold Story of the Persian Gulf War*, New York: Houghton Mifflin, p. 217

"Would earn them seats in the dock at Nuremburg"

Noam Chomsky, "If the Nuremberg laws were applied, then every post-war American president would have been hanged." Lecture delivered, 1990. This contention sometimes provokes the response, 'What about Jimmy Carter?' as if he was exempt. His defenders overlook Carter's determination, in collaboration with his secretary of State, Brzezinski, to "give the Soviet Union its very own Vietnam" by arming the Mujahedeen in Afghanistan and encouraging them to kill Russians with US supplied Stinger missiles.

"Claiming it was anthrax and thus a pretext for war"

"It was the information that we had. We provided it. If that information is inaccurate, fine."

US Secretary of State Colin Powell comments on the statement by IAEA Director General

Mohamed El Baradei that the US had supplied forged documents claiming Iraq was attempting to acquire uranium. March 9, 2003

"The man who torched Vietnamese villages with his Zippo lighter."

In *My American Journey*, Powell recounted his reaction when he spotted his first dead Viet Cong. "He lay on his back, gazing up at us with sightless eyes," Powell wrote. "I felt nothing, certainly not sympathy. I had seen too much death and suffering on our side to care anything about what happened on theirs."

While success against the armed enemy was rare, Powell's ARVN unit punished the civilian population systematically. As the soldiers marched through mountainous jungle, they destroyed the food and the homes of the region's Montagnards, who were suspected of sympathizing with the Viet Cong. Old women would cry hysterically as their ancestral homes and worldly possessions were consumed by fire.

For nearly six months, Powell and his ARVN unit slogged through the jungles, searching for Viet Cong and destroying villages."

"Your enemy or starved him to death?"

Colin Powell, *My American Journey*, Ballantine Books, 2003

"It is not an American concern".

http://www.nytimes.com/2010/12/11/us/politics/11nixon.html

"In the campaign to secure Iraqi oil assets."

'MANAMA, Bahrain - U.S. Navy Captain John Peterson shares a light-hearted moment with His Royal Highness Prince Andrew Jan. 25. Prince Andrew presented Peterson with the prestigious Honorary Order of the British Empire for his leadership of coalition forces, which included a large number of Royal Navy Sailors and Marines, "in the campaign to secure Iraqi oil assets", during the onset of Operation Iraqi Freedom in 2003.' US Navy picture archives, 2003

"…four hundred horses are annually shot for the Queen's hobby;

Since the start of Race Horse Death Watch, on 13th March 2007, 1302 racetrack deaths have been recorded over 3089 Days, http://www.horsedeathwatch.com/

"For princely players wearing harsh metal spurs."

Nick Fagge, 'Prince Harry faces animal cruelty claim over polo pony's stab wound from his spur,' London: *Daily Mail*, 3rd September 2010

"Which royal guards wear in sentry boxes while saving their Queen."

The practice provoked a letter to the Times from the singer Morrissey. It was headed, 'Hats are not worth killing for: guards wearing real fur reflects the human spirit at its lowest' Morrissey told Times readers "The mere sight of each bearskin hat must surely jab at the Queen's heart", *The Times*, 3 August, 2010   Morrissey's letter evidently left the royal heart un-jabbed since the custom continues, with the Ministry of Defense claiming to be unable to find a substitute that is acceptable to the Palace – given its adherence to tradition this is, in this particularly case, quite literally hidebound.

"a sort of weird aristocratic fertility rite."

Tanya Gold, 'Royal wedding: The agony of the ecstasy', *The Guardian*, 25 November 2011

"Ortet was rounded on as a 'fucking frog.'"

Ingrid Seward, *William and Harry: a portrait of two princes*, Headline, 2003. p.240

"Just by manipulating her genitalia."

Peter Dominiczak and Emer Martin, 'First glimpse inside the exclusive nude show club where Prince Harry partied,' London: *Evening Standard*, 18 Feb 2011

"…he gave Prince Charles an Aston Martin"

Phillip Hall, *Royal Fortune: Tax, Money and the Monarchy*, London, Bloomsbury, 1992, p.184

"While they discuss a wedding that stiffs the public for twenty million"

'Kate's foie gras lunch with Camilla: But what would Charles say about 'cruel' dish', by Fay Schlesinger, John Stevens and Tamara Cohen, *Daily Mail*, 15 February 2011

"Giving them fifteen percent more of Crown Estate profits."

Fay Schlesinger, 'Britain's Royal Family to rake-in Millions extra as rest of Country suffers swingeing Government cuts,' London: *Daily Mail*, 22 October 2010

SOURCES PAGES 33-40

"Would set up an ordinary commonwealth."

This is, in fact, an indirect quote: "Johnson [a royalist] knew that Milton was a republican, he says, 'an acrimonious and surly republican for which it is not known that he gave any better reason, than that a popular government is the most frugal; for the trappings of a monarchy would set up an ordinary commonwealth" Arthur Murphy, from *An Essay on the life and genius of Samuel Johnson LLD*, London: Longmans, White and Sons, 1792, p. 180

"the string that holds a robber's bundle".

'Monarchy is only the string which ties the robber's bundle.' Shelley first wrote this in an essay 'A Philosophical View of Reform', which was composed between November 1819 and 20 May 1820. The sentence would be used as a headline for the Socialist Worker's coverage of the Royal Jubilee of Queen Elizabeth in 1977.

"Very rare, very sparing and very respectful."

http://www.bbc.co.uk/news/uk-politics-12604190

"(In the hope that his other massages go away)."

Rebecca English, 'The tarnished medal: After those linked with a paedophile, was this the right time for the Queen to honour Andrew?' London: *Daily Mail*, 30 March, 2011

With a convicted paedophile and tyrannical foreign regimes,"

77 'Seven medals Andy? That's a princely sum: The Duke's gongs are revealed' *Daily Mail*, 31 March 2011

"The Queen makes him a Knight Grand Cross of the Royal Victorian Order,"

http://www.dailymail.co.uk/news/article-1371367/Prince-Andrew-given-Knight-Grand-Cross-Queen-Jeffrey-Epstein-paedophile-link.html#ixzz1Iemo8irN

"By child-unfriendly bombs made by Royal Ordnance"

BAE Systems Global Combat Systems Munitions. Incorporates Royal Ordnance at Fazakerley in Liverpool, manufacturers of DU shells

"Who all live worse than any English beggar."

Jonathan Swift, *A Short View of the State of Ireland*, 1730

"Of using poisoned gas against uncivilized tribes."

Winston S. Churchill: departmental minute (Churchill papers: 16/16) 12 May 1919 War Office from Companion Volume 4, Part 1 of the official biography, *Winston S. Churchill*, by Martin Gilbert London: Heinemann, 1976

"With the representative of the King-Emperor."

Martin Gilbert, *Churchill: The Wilderness Years*, Houghton Mifflin, 1984, p. 34

"And killing them with total impunity."

A POWERFUL Panorama TV documentary last week uncovered the shocking truth about the British establishment's bloody role in Northern Ireland. "A Licence to Kill" showed how the British army and security forces worked hand in glove with the most sectarian and violent Loyalist terrorists. It revealed that the top brass of the British army and Northern Ireland's sectarian police force, the RUC (now renamed the Police Service of Northern Ireland), colluded with Loyalist terror gangs to murder Catholics.

FORCE RESEARCH UNIT (FRU), One of the British army's most secret units, which infiltrated Loyalist paramilitary gangs, passing them names of Catholics to be targeted. According to the Guardian, "The FRU is still operating, albeit under a different name."

Hazel Croft, How British state used death squads,' *Socialist Worker*, Issue: 1806 dated: 29 June 2002

"And he implied it was beneath his notice."

Maria Misra, lecturer in modern history at Keble College, Oxford 'Heart of smugness: Unlike Belgium, Britain is still complacently ignoring the gory cruelties of its empire', *The Guardian*, 23 July 2002

An heir once let slip, "I don't want to be King."

Ingrid Seward, op cit p. 194

"Democracy...is the deadliest enemy to a monarchy"

Sir Julius Caesar (sic), Chancellor of the Exchequer (1606-14) to James I "Democracy... is the deadliest enemy to a monarchy"

"Is celebrated in subversive songs as a hero"

Michael Fagan broke into Buckingham Palace in the early hours of 9 July 1982 and entered

Elizabeth II's bedroom, prompting a number of football chants sung by Scottish, Irish and Welsh supporters to provoke English football fans. These alleged that Fagan's brief encounter with the Queen was to their mutual satisfaction.

"To be used as pawns for foreign policy,"

Henry Kissinger, quoted by Bob Woodward in *The Final Days*, 1976

"Useful, as in racing, to those buying and selling."

Scott Thomson, "The Ultimate Insider Trader is the Queen" *Executive Intelligence Review*, Volume 23, Number 22, May 24, 1996, p 73.

"And the Queen was advised to invest in uranium"

The Queen opened the world's first full-scale nuclear power station, at Calder Hall in Cumberland. BBC News, 17th October, 1956

Cf. also Nuclear News: The News That Matters about the Nuclear Industry, September 28, 2015

"An unashamed member of Hitler Youth"

Leuren Moret, *Who is profiting from this global uranium nightmare?* American Free Press - Issue #10/11, March 6 & 13, 2006

"This was company policy, 'to reduce theft.'"

'Tiny Rowland, The Ugly Face of Neocolonialism in Africa', Washington: *Executive Intelligence Review*, 1993, p. 120

Are now worth more than six billion dollars

Leuren Moret , Hiroshima To Iraq - 61 Years Of Uranium Wars A Suicidal, Genocidal, Omnicidal Course, *San Francisco Bay View:* Global Research, October 9, 2007

"Lonrho has a stake in Brinkley Mining, a growing player in the re-emerging market for the uranium that fuels nuclear power stations." Tom Stevenson, 'Africa benefits as Lonrho bounces back', London: *Daily Telegraph*, 4 Apr 2007

Depleted Uranium has turned the worms mutant.

Jasper Hamill,'Depleted uranium turns earthworms into glowworms' Fears that radioactive material has tainted ecosystem. *Herald Scotland*, 15 Mar 2008,

"The silent killer that will never stop killing"

http://www.sovereignindependent. com/?p=16394

"A billionaire with an income from grave robbing."

http://www.guardian.co.uk/uk/2002/ may/30/politics.jubilee

"Which is," she despaired, "obsessed with royalty."

Kitty Kelley, op cit., p. xiii

"To protect this precious superstition from satire."

Stephen Bates,'Council's refusal to let it hold a street party is politically motivated,' *The Guardian*, 11 April 2011

"Said Canada was 'a good investment'"

Kitty Kelly, op. cit. p. 94

"Often hidden behind surrogate names."

"…the reason for the wild variations in valuations of her private wealth can be pinned on the secrecy over her portfolio of share investments. This is because her subjects have no way of knowing through a public register of interests where she, as their head of state, chooses to invest her money. Unlike the members of the Commons and now the Lords, the Queen does not have to annually declare her interests and as a result her subjects cannot question her or know about potential conflicts of interests..."

"Horses, stamps, cars - and an invisible portfolio: Private assets valued at up to £1.15bn" *The Guardian*, Thursday 30 May 2002

"A mechanized automaton."

P. B. Shelley, Queen Mab, Book III

"(In what are squalid race wars over resources)."

Gordon Rayner, 'Prince William still determined to fight in Afghanistan. Prince William will not allow married life to get in the way of his continued determination to serve in Afghanistan, The Telegraph has learnt. Prince William is expected to put in a fresh request for a tour of duty in Afghanistan' London: *Daily Telegraph*, 22 Apr 2011

"Are paid ninety-nine pence an hour."

Fay Schlesinger, 'Kate's dazzling dress is made in Romanian 'sweatshop' by women on just 99p an hour', *Daily Mail*, 28 May 2011